PERE MARQUETTE STATE PARK

JERSEY COUNTY, ILLINOIS

An Unofficial Guide to History, Natural History, Trails, and Drives

T0083733

PERE MARQUETTE STATE PARK

Founded in 1932, this 8050 acre park is now the largest natural landscape state park in Illinois. Rare for Illinois, the park covers one of the few unglaciated areas in the state. The resulting rugged topography exposes many limestone cliffs and outcrops. The unusually rich flora includes plants of upland and ravine forests, and hill prairies, a vegetation type originally very widespread in Illinois.

▢ **Park Boundaries**   ▬ **Roads**

P **Parking Lot**

Trails

= Goat Cliff	= Hickory North
= Dogwood	= Hickory South
= Ridge	= Fern Hollow
= Ravine	= Rattlesnake
= Hickory	= Oak

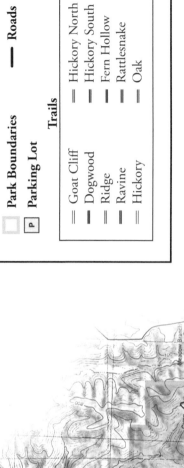

Acknowledgments

Over the years numerous companions shared park explorations and inspired curiosity, especially: Jody, Philip, and Gordon Keating, Jim Fralish, Dick Worthen, Gayle Borman, Jill Mellenthin, Bob Freeman, Sandra Wood, Jim Bensman, Steve Sands, and Glennon Tockstein. Most, not coincidentally, were also fellow members of the Alton-based Piasa Palisades Group of the Sierra Club. Through the 1970s and 1980s I often walked with Bruce Quackenbush, who led interesting monthly hikes throughout the park.

The manuscript was improved by the editing of some parts by Natalia Coleridge, and the initial copy editing by Ellen Kunkelmann. At the Missouri Botanical Garden Press I am grateful for the able reviews by Lisa Pepper and Amanda Koehler, and for the final editing by Managing Editor Allison Brock. Kurt Tiede's able graphics work improved the maps and geology illustrations. I am grateful to then Press Director Victoria Hollowell for her early encouragement of the project, and to Liz Fathman, Director of Print and Digital Media at the Missouri Botanical Garden.

As the manuscript progressed, members of the park administration were supportive and encouraging. These include Chris Hespen, Site Superintendent, who also gave me access to the park history files. Thanks also to Scott Isringhausen, former Park Naturalist, and Janelle Volger, public face of park management, for their help and enthusiasm.

Pam Warford, then Assistant Site Superintendent, was generous with her time and deep knowledge of the region's history. In the early stages of this project, staff members of the Jersey County Historical Society, Jerseyville, and at the Illinois State Archives, Springfield, generously provided files that clarified much interesting history.

I cannot end this section without expressing my gratitude for the fact that this park exists. The publication in your hands was only conceivable because of rare vision ranging from local enthusiasts to the federal government. It began with the energy of newspaper editors John D. McAdams and Joe Page, and many state officials, including the governor. Federal agencies such as the National Park Service and the Civilian Conservation Corps made substantial contributions. The amazing part is that it was accomplished expeditiously in the depths of the Great Depression. What would be the chances today?

QUICK PARK FACTS

- **Founding:** Pere Marquette State Park, at original dedication in 1932, consisted of about 1500 acres. A few years later National Park Service purchases added the St. Andrew ridge tract to the north. Through subsequent acquisitions by the state, the park has since grown to about 8050 acres, making it Illinois' largest protected natural landscape.

- **Early human history:** The region was long considered by original peoples to be a resource-rich environment. About 12,000 years of continuously evolving human culture are documented in this region.

- **Historic times:** In September 1673, Joliet and Marquette were the first Europeans to see these bluffs and the adjacent Illinois River. Traders seeking beaver pelts followed for several decades, but settlement was sparse due to malaria. Settlers in the park area arrived about 1821. The settlement that became Grafton was platted in 1836.

- **Geology:** The local bedrock is Paleozoic, calcareous and sedimentary. Pleistocene glacial advances produced no ice cover over the park, but deep wind-blown soil, called loess, blanketed the uplands.

- **Climate:** The annual temperature range (cold to hot) is over 100°F, causing the area to be considered a "continental climate."

- **Precipitation:** The annual range is 35–40 inches, distributed in all months, but with significant annual variation.
- **Topography:** From river level (419 feet) to highest point in the park (892 feet), the total relief is 473 feet. The typical range, valley to ridge, is about 300 feet.
- **Soils:** Seven types are present, ranging from prairie to forest soil development.
- **Ecological communities:** Five community types are present, based on elevation, exposure, and moisture availability.
- **Plants:** More than 460 species of vascular plants, belonging to 102 families, are present.
- **Animals:** There are about 59 reptile and amphibian species, 46 mammal species, and 234 species of birds.

CHAPTER 1

PARK AMENITIES

The following information introduces the public face of the park. Much more information, regularly updated, can be accessed through websites and contact information listed after the various topics. There are two management epicenters: park administration and concession-operated activity centers.

The park administration includes a site superintendent and staff, which are under the jurisdiction of the Illinois Department of Natural Resources (IDNR). Contact information: Pere Marquette State Park, 13112 Visitor Center Lane, Grafton, IL 62037. Tel: 618-786-3323. Also, the IDNR website is quite detailed: www.dnr.state.il.us/lands/landmgt/parks.

MUSEUM AND VISITOR CENTER

This fine facility is across the Scenic Drive entrance and to the northwest of the lodge complex. On entering the park's main entrance, the first left turn takes you into the visitor center parking lot. The visitor center was built in 1997 and features a small museum that describes the area's Native American heritage and introduces the wildlife. Also of great interest in the main room is a recently installed large, raised relief map of the park. One can get a feel for the roads and trails, their topography, views, and type of scenery. A staff member is available to field questions, and a rack of brochures and maps is available. The visitor center is closed on Sundays and state holidays.

A popular program operating December through March is Bald Eagle Days. Weekly programs begin in the morning with a video shown at the visitor center. Participants then drive to sites to observe eagles. Call the visitor center for the schedule.

The second epicenter of activities, described below, is operated by concessions under state contract.

THE PERE MARQUETTE LODGE, CONFERENCE CENTER, AND CABINS

Where Route 100 turns to the north along the Illinois River stands the lodge, a unique architectural treasure. The center section of this elongated structure was built between 1933 and 1939 by the Civilian Conservation Corps (CCC) during the Roosevelt Administration's "New Deal" programs. The original building, built at a cost of just over $350,000, was dedicated and opened to the public in 1940. It was renovated and substantially enlarged in 1988.

Aerial view of lodge. The stressed lawn is due to a dry fall.

As you enter the lobby, you go back in history a century. Beginning in Victorian times, the erection of extravagant hotels of wood and stone, as seen also in Yellowstone and Glacier National Parks, and in western Canada, became known as the "grand lodge" style. Some have called it "parkitecture," and it represents a now-vanished era of construction history. Gazing upward you note the wood. Supporting the roof are massive pillars, carved from the trunks of Douglas fir, western cedar, and cypress.

Most of the other materials are of local origin. At one end of the main hall stands the 50-foot-high, 700-ton fireplace of Silurian dolomite, which was quarried in nearby Grafton. This especially dense stone was also used to build the walls on the seven nearby cabins that stand upslope from the lodge. The unique and massive wooden furniture was crafted by Illinois prison inmates of the era. Much of the metalwork, from the beautiful chandeliers to door handles and window locks, was crafted by skilled CCC specialists. In front of the fireplace stands the unique life-sized chess board with waist-high chess pieces.

FACILITIES

There are 50 guest rooms in the lodge and 22 in the adjacent cottages. Each of the cottages features three separate guest rooms. On the second floor of the original building, the vintage but updated rooms, which opened for occupancy in 1940, are accessible by stairs. The new south wing, built in 1988, features a pool atrium and guest rooms accessible by elevator. The north wing includes a conference center with all of the resources needed for small or large gatherings. The lodge also hosts the Mary Michelle Winery and a gift shop. There are numerous events throughout the year, for which the website should be consulted.

Contact information: Pere Marquette Lodge and Conference Center, Route 100, P.O. Box 429, Grafton, IL 62037. Tel: 618-786-2331. Fax: 618-786-3498. Website: www.pmlodge.net. E-mail: thelodge@gtec.com.

PICNIC AREAS

There are four picnic shelters. Three are across from the main entrance to the park, on the river side. Inside the entrance to the campground is a fourth picnic pavilion and comfort station. Groups can reserve the shelters in advance by calling the visitor center. The campground entrance is off Route 100, just to the east of the main entrance of the park. On the ridge, along the Upper Park Road, are several picnic areas and comfort stations.

Riverside shelter. This and several other features of the park are found on the west side of the highway, across from the lodge.

BOAT HARBOR

Along the river, off Route 100 to the west and across from the park's main entrance, are launching ramps, boat docks, and ample car parking. Day use of the docks is free, but overnight use requires paying a camping fee.

HUNTING

This activity occurs on 2000 acres off Graham Hollow Road, plus 1344 acres at Copperhead Hollow Wildlife Area to the north. Each year the IDNR publishes the dates and regulations. Archery hunting is allowed on 3000 acres of the St. Andrew ridge in the neighborhood of the three organized group camps. There are four 8-day seasons for turkey hunting. For more information, see the IDNR website. Permit office tel: 217-782-7305.

DRIVES AND TRAILS

See relevant chapters.

PUBLIC CAMPGROUND

Billed as a "class A" campground, the site is reached from Route 100 (the River Road) and located just east of the lodge complex. It is operated by a park concession and is open year-round. It features an exceptional layout with 80 well-spaced grassy sites, none of which are pull-through. The roads are paved, and two of the sites are handicapped accessible. Most of the back-in gravel pads are level across the axle.

Aerial view of campground, showing the RV parking area near the highway. The site is just to the east of the lodge parking area.

Electrical hookups are available, with some featuring 50-amp service. About five water spigots are scattered around the campground. There are two rustic rent-a-cabins on shaded sites. Uphill from the class A campground is a tent camping area, without numbered sites.

Campsites closest to the road are in an open area. But further back, many sites border the perimeter woods or are shaded by mature trees. Sites 2 through 30 are reservable online, while the remaining sites are available on a first-come, first-served basis. All sites have access to the shower building. Reservable sites, rent-a-cabins, and picnic shelters can be scheduled through: www.reserveamerica.com.

Tent camping area at the back of the main campground.

As you arrive, the location of the campground host in site 1 is clearly marked. The host is present May through October, 7 days a week. Maps of the campground layout are available. One can register at the visitor center during normal business hours. After hours, or when the host is absent, the location of reserved sites is not obvious.

The shower building, open April 1 through mid-December, is ample sized and clean. In the wash basin section, the water taps are spring-loaded; no washing both hands at once. Also, there are no shelves for placing toiletries, or hooks on which to hang a towel. This lack of practicality is by no means unique to Illinois campgrounds.

DUNCAN HILL YOUTH TENT CAMP

This site can be reserved for groups of young people and their leaders, using the previously mentioned campground website. A picnic shelter, tables, pit toilets, and drinking water are available. Heading north out of Grafton, the entrance driveway on the right is 1.1 miles past the Brussels Ferry entrance or 1.7 miles east of the park's main entrance.

GROUP CAMPS OUATOGA, PIASA, AND POTAWATOMIE

These camps are available to groups by advance reservation, but applications should be submitted promptly each year after January 1. Each camp consists of a number of primitive cabins, some larger cabins with fireplaces, a modern comfort station, and a dining hall with equipped kitchen. Contact the site superintendent's office for more detailed information on facilities and application submission.

Group camp Ouatoga. One of three such areas, these original Civilian Conservation Corps–built cabins are being renovated by volunteers from the local Sierra Club group and The Nature Institute.

BACKPACKING

There are no backcountry sites or routes. All camping must be done in designated campgrounds.

BIKE TRAIL

The 20-mile Sam Vadalabene Bike Trail runs from the lodge grounds along Route 100, past the bluffs and the river, ending at Alton. The ample parking area just west of Alton includes a comfort station and also features a re-creation of the Piasa Bird painted on the limestone bluffs. The bike trail is entirely paved but is only separated from the highway along parts of the route. Care must be taken at several road crossings.

EQUESTRIAN ACTIVITIES

A concession, Pere Marquette Riding Stables, offers guided trail rides daily except Tuesdays. The operation is open May through October, or extended earlier in the spring or later in the fall depending on weather. The facility is open 10:00 am to 4:00 pm and is available from Route 100. Heading west, the entrance, on the right, is 0.6 mile beyond the Brussels Ferry entrance. It is 2.2 miles east of the park's main entrance. Horses are available and are best reserved in advance. Check with the concessionaire or the visitor center for details. There are about 2.5 miles of horse trails that offer a 45- to 50-minute ride. Evening hayrides are also available by reservation. For more information, call: 618-786-2156.

For those who bring their horses, public-access trailer parking can be reached through Graham Hollow Road, which is 1.4 miles east of the riding stables off Route 100. On entering Graham Hollow Road, find the driveway to the parking area, soon appearing on the left. There are surrounding horse trails, which may also be used by hikers.

CHAPTER 2

PARK HISTORY AND FOUNDING

The story begins in the early years of the Great Depression. By 1931, hard times and financial distress were widespread among farm families in the heavily wooded west end of Jersey County. It was especially difficult for those whose properties included the hills and valleys of what is now Pere Marquette State Park. Even in good times, farming operations had been marginal due to the hilly landscape and the isolation caused by inadequate farm-to-market roads. When these conditions were combined with the general downturn of the economy, very little incentive remained for staying on the land.

Throughout this time many citizens of the region shared an appreciation of the unique beauty of this cliff-bordered bend in the Mississippi and Illinois Rivers. Among visionary citizens of the region, two local newspaper editors and civic leaders have each been suggested as originator of the idea of establishing a state park. The first, known as "Uncle Joe" Page, was a Civil War veteran and editor of the *Jersey County Democrat*. The other was John D. McAdams, publisher of the *Alton Telegraph*. As an aside, John was the son of William McAdams, Jr., an active 19th-century archeologist who, no doubt, inculcated a love of the region in his son John. Later, the high point known as McAdams Peak was named in honor of William.

John McAdams and Joe Page worked as an effective team to establish a State Park Committee in 1931. McAdams, who signed his letters "Chairman of the State Park Committee," hit upon the idea of raising matching funds to buy out willing sellers in the area. McAdams took the lead in contacting the state officials who became instrumental to making the park happen on the state level. H. H. Cleaveland, Director of the Department of Public Works and Buildings in Springfield, and Robert Kingery, Secretary of the Board of Park Advisors in Chicago, both supported the project from an early stage. McAdams carried on a detailed and lengthy correspondence with state officials to keep them informed as he set up the matching part of the proposal.

SUCCESSFUL FUND DRIVE

The speed at which such projects could be accomplished in those days certainly stands in contrast with today's glacial pace. On July 10, 1931, McAdams started the campaign to raise $25,000. While McAdams worked on raising contributions in Madison County, Page agreed to solicit funds from citizens in the Jersey County area. With strong support from some local industrialists and bankers, as well as smaller gifts from many local citizens, the Madison County fundraising was quite successful in 1931–1932. Park fundraising did less well in the more rural Jersey County, as family farmers and small businesses had little discretionary cash in those days. Also, by unfortunate timing, an $80,000 fund drive was underway in Jersey County to help the unemployed.

For the park acquisition the plan was to raise $25,000, which was to be matched by the state to provide the necessary funds to purchase the land. In the end the local effort topped out at $23,085, which was matched by legislative appropriation for a total of $46,270.

Simultaneously with the fundraising, McAdams and his committee worked tirelessly to negotiate with landowners. A well-connected local citizen, George Brainerd, was instrumental in making many of these contacts. By all accounts, most were relieved if not delighted to be selling their land. In some cases, unpaid back taxes constituted a lien on their properties. Nineteen families agreed to sell for the "Jersey County Park" (also called the "Grafton State Park") project. Most of these families owned 40- to 180-acre tracts and were offered a range of $300 to $11,000, with an average price of $2435, or about $23 per acre for their properties.

McAdams held a meeting with landowners in early May 1932. On May 6, he had written to Dr. C. M. Service of the Department of Public Works in Springfield: "This is going to be a wonderful meeting. We are going to distribute $49,000 or $50,000 to a company of people who have not seen any real money for a long time. Just think what a big day it will be for these people. And, also, be kind enough to think of what a big day it will be for 'yours truly' who has worked for over a year and slept and dreamed on this park. It means my labor is done and project succeeds. Yours truly, John D. McAdams."

A LIVELY CORRESPONDENCE

Some of the correspondence gives the flavor of the times:

McAdams to Cleaveland (June 6, 1931): "A native up in that country the other day entertained me with a story about three spring lambs that wandered down to the creek in Mason Hollow. A bootlegger's mash vat had broken and the mash was flowing in the creek. The spring lambs drank freely and afterwards ran up the bluffs and chased two fine Holstein bulls over the bluff."

McAdams to Cleaveland (August 18, 1931): "An old native of Grafton who heard that I suffered with stomach trouble, sent me a bottle of something which he made which he says will cure anything. I took a good whiff of it and corked it up again and wrote him to try to raise some of those seventy two barrels of pre Civil War liquor from the sands of the river and send me a few bottles of that."

McAdams to Cleaveland (August 25, 1931): "Had a visitor last Saturday, hardest looking customer I have seen for a long time. Said he was a fisherman up on Illinois and said if I would tip him off where those seventy two barrels of Civil War whiskey are buried he would get 'em out for half. So I may send you a barrel after all. Give it to some of those labor fellows up there who want to hold up the road paving." (The *Alton Telegraph* had reported on August 15, 1931: "Hard roads celebration in Grafton: formal opening of hard road from route 3 to Grafton and public jubilee thereafter.")

McAdams to Cleaveland (July 18, 1931, after saying he probably could only come up with $12,000): "Jersey County has failed me almost completely up to this time. There are very few people in the county who could afford to give liberally." Fortunately, in the coming months, McAdams was able to raise most of the money from bankers and industrialists in the Alton area.

McAdams to Service (May 2, 1932): "I do not know how I am going to wait till we get some auto roads up in to this park and up to where it is, but guess I will have to be patient. The park will be a humdinger and you can lay to that."

The *Illinois State Register* reported that May 19, 1932, was chosen by Director Cleaveland for transfer of properties to the state because it was the 87th birthday of "Uncle Joe" Page, editor of the *Jersey County Democrat*, member of the state board of highway advisors, and principal Jersey County booster of the park project. It added, "Following his usual custom [Joe Page] will entertain several hundred children at a Jerseyville theatre."

The meeting was arranged by McAdams, Chairman of the committee; Hugh W. Cross, Jerseyville, Secretary; and C. A. Caldwell, Alton, Treasurer. The highway department agreed to a survey to determine the position of roadways.

Governor Louis L. Emmerson approved the park board's recommendation because of the area's history with early explorers; Indian battles; hundreds of mounds; its elevations and vistas of rare beauty; the presence of at least 25 springs with pure, sparkling water; the accessibility to citizens of Jersey and surrounding counties; and the growing need for recreation centers.

NAMING OF THE PARK

As land acquisition was under way, state officials solicited suggestions from citizens to name the new state park. Park literature states that the park was named by "popular demand," but calling it an organized drive would be more accurate. All during the summer of 1932, suggestions for naming the park went to Director Cleaveland in Springfield. The volume of cards and letters received indicated a lively interest in this process. "Piasa Bluffs Park" had local support, as did "Blackhawk State Park," "Lincoln Memorial Park," "McAdams State Park," and "Illini State Park."

Pere Marquette. A bronze sculpture of the Jesuit priest/explorer stands across from the lodge entrance. It was created by artist Kirk St. Maur.

The winning nomination resulted from a petition campaign organized by the Knights of Columbus. At least 12 chapters of the Catholic organization, including local east-side chapters, sent in copies of a petition initiated by the Chicago chapter. The petition proposed that the park be named as it came to be, since it was at this site where "Pere Marquette, intrepid and priestly explorer first entered the state of Illinois... No similar honor has been paid to the man so largely responsible for the exploration of the great Middle West, and who risked his life that the joys of Christianity and gifts of civilization might be brought to the Indian." Unfortunately, absent is any mention of Louis Jolliet. Historical reports note that, for exploring enterprise, Jolliet was appointed as expedition leader by civilian authorities. Its principal purpose was exploration, and to determine whether the Mississippi River emptied into the Gulf of Mexico or into the Gulf of California.*

Copies of this petition, in the form of a resolution, were sent to Governor Emmerson on October 18, 1932. The governor decided on "Pere Marquette State Park" because, as Director Cleaveland noted, it was supported by the greatest number of people.

---

*In fairness, it should be noted that we only have Marquette's journals. Near the journey's end, Jolliet's canoe overturned in rapids, and boxes of maps, diaries, and other papers were lost.

Earlier that August, Paul B. Cousley, editor of the *Alton Telegraph*, wrote to C. M. Service in Springfield, that a "descriptive name would be preferred, but if none can be decided upon, then the name of Marquette would be recognizing an early explorer."

John McAdams wrote to C. M. Service on May 24, 1932, to nominate Mr. George Brainerd, assessor of Quarry township, as a candidate for custodian of the state park. McAdams noted that he knows the land, the crops, and the people. The selling of crops and fruits would yield most of the money needed to pay the custodian. McAdams had previously written to Robert Kingery, Secretary to the Board of Park Advisors, Chicago, on July 27, 1931: "...Brainerd has accomplished a good piece of work. He knows all these people and to get contiguous lands through the section could not have been accomplished by anyone else I know."

THE INFRASTRUCTURE, U.S. NATIONAL PARK SERVICE, AND THE CIVILIAN CONSERVATION CORPS

When the park project seemed likely to succeed, local officials negotiated with the National Park Service for much of the required building. Their willingness to take on the project in the 1930s, supervising the work of the Civilian Conservation Corps (CCC), accelerated the development of the park by a decade. Work crews from throughout Illinois, organized as the 1646th company, were in place beginning in the spring of 1933. Housed at Camp Gram in Graham Hollow, the men worked 40-hour weeks, completing their work on the lodge and other structures by June 30, 1939.

"Camp Gram" housed one of the Civilian Conservation Corps units that built park infrastructure. Sited on the east slope of Graham Hollow, the present forest hides the few remains.

In addition to the lodge, the hundreds of other structures included barns, roads, bridges, houses, check dams, pipelines, garages, latrines, and numerous other objects. The stone rip-rap seen frequently in the woods in many locations all date from the CCC era. Corps workers also accomplished the planting of 300,000 trees and shrubs. According to records, many of the campground features were built by the CCC as well as 18 miles of foot trails. Simultaneously, alongside infrastructure work, hundreds of man-days were spent assessing the park region for the presence of important native burial grounds.

In the early 1930s, while the main infrastructure was being built on the southern acreage, an organization of the federal government, the Relief Administration, was proposing to add about 2500 acres to the park on the north end, which had not been part of the original vision. The proposing study called it the "Pere Marquette submarginal land area," which is known today as the St. Andrew ridge, and the site of the group camps Ouatoga and Piasa. "Submarginal": what a name for a beautiful collection of big trees, and views with an Appalachian-like feel! But, up through the 1950s, "conservation" mostly had to do with utility—its highest use for man, in this case agriculture, for which it was "submarginal." The study proposal suggested that group camps be erected especially to enhance the outdoor experience of "large groups of underprivileged, yet happy and eager children" from St. Louis. "The physical and mental benefits gained by the children during their stay in these delightful and beautiful surroundings will be gratifying to observe, and the permanent good such outings will do for these youngsters will be reflected in a more healthy and robust future generation." So said the report's author, J. Howard Kane. Indeed, an eternal truth.

Properties were gradually purchased from willing landowners at about $10 per acre. As the two group camps were being constructed, this northern adjacent acreage, called the St. Andrew ridge, was officially a Federal Recreation and Demonstration Area. Later it was added to Pere Marquette State Park by the National Park Board in Washington, D.C., making the park, at 4000 acres, the largest Illinois state park.

While the first CCC company worked on the original landscape, an additional company, the 1637th, centered their labors on construction of the organized group camps, named Camp Piasa and Camp Ouatoga. Since those days they have served as rustic facilities for the recreation of mostly urban families from the surrounding region. Mostly completed around 1937, there were 60 cabins, two mess halls, two swimming pools, and several staff cabins. The original structures are mostly still in use, but many are in need of rehabilitation. Today, among Grafton-area residents are those whose fathers and grandfathers were rescued from unemployment and poverty by becoming part of this park's construction history.

DEDICATION OF THE LODGE

The magnificent stone lodge was built on the Brussels terrace, a river alluvium of Pleistocene age, and dedicated on May 4, 1941. The afternoon dedication ceremony was a major crowd event and included many speeches. Among the seven speakers, Governor Dwight H. Green gave an inspiring talk on the theme: "In gatherings such as this, we can meet in supreme liberty and give thanks that government still must serve its people." Walter A. Rosenfield, Director of Public Works and Buildings, pointed out that "Illinois was among the first states to make use of the CCC on state park property." He noted that the development of this park was one of the largest and most complex projects undertaken by the Corps anywhere in the United States. By the time of this dedication, John D. McAdams was deceased.

As Rosenfield continued, "The peak at the west end of the park is named for the late John D. McAdams' father [William McAdams, Jr.], geologist of national reputation, who spent much time exploring the site and recommended it as a park long ago." While the original tract included 1550 acres, by 1941 it exceeded 1760 acres. Great credit is due to the National Park Service. The lodge was made possible and the development program was advanced at least 10 years.

The lodge great room. Built by the Civilian Conservation Corps in the 1930s, this impressive structure features the huge 700-ton fireplace and heavy furniture built by Illinois prison inmates of that period.

"The opening of the lodge with its native limestone, its massive timbers, and its great lounge, signalizes completion of a major project in a program to make Pere Marquette State Park an outstanding example of Illinois' rapid progress toward national leadership in the field of recreational planning."

The program booklet acknowledged, "The Div. of Parks and Memorials especially appreciates the valuable assistance of the Civilian Conservation Corps working under the guidance of the National Park Service in construction of the lodge and its companion structures." Also thanked were the "residents of Jersey County who have for many years unselfishly labored for the park's development and betterment..."

Several vacation areas, called group camps, were built in 1948. They had been started by the National Park Service and left incomplete, but they were finished by the state at a cost of about $50,000. Later, in 1985, the north and south wings of the lodge were added.

PARK ODDITIES

THE PARK AND THE COLD WAR (1955–1975)

In the Cold War era the U.S. government, being seriously worried about the nation's vulnerability to attack from Soviet Russia, decided to emplace state-of-the-art missile defenses in the vicinity of population centers throughout the United States. From coast to coast, about 300 sites were developed to launch Nike-Ajax or Nike-Hercules surface-to-air missiles.

Being near St. Louis, Pere Marquette State Park caught the eye of officials as ideal for placing a missile battery, even though the Division of Parks preferred it be elsewhere. The Army wanted the site because it: "...would be to best advantage of Army in case it became necessary to defend the St. Louis area."

Construction of the Nike Missile Base atop the hills in Marquette Park was going forward on schedule, with a completion date of June 1959. The base, being built by Fruin Colnon Co. of St. Louis, would cost almost $2 million. The Army would install the mechanism for firing and handling the Nike Hercules and Nike Ajax missiles. The photo shows one of three launching bins being built. The base would be part of a missile-launching ring designed to protect the area from an aerial attack. Telegraph archive photo from the collection of Jeanette Pauley.

Nike Missile Base. During the Cold War, about 1959, this facility was constructed on the southern portion of St. Andrew ridge. The remains of the base are closed to the public.

For the military, ideal sites were elevated and had deep soil and little rock, so the heavily loess-covered bluffs at the southern end of the St. Andrew ridge filled the bill. For a 10-year period beginning in 1958, the army leased 26 acres of the then-6000-acre park as Nike Site SL-90. A decade later, on December 10, 1968, the short-lived base was shut down. Beginning around 1965, intercontinental ballistic missiles led to the obsolescence of the Nike system.

These days, in the vicinity of Upper Park Road and the turn-off to Camp Potawatomi, the slab foundations of barracks remain visible behind a chain-link fence. The barracks had a short life as a state ecological training center before that useful activity was unfunded by the state. Just to the east is an overgrown chain-link fence leading to the entombed set of 25-foot-deep silos whose contents once aimed to protect American polity.

A Midwestern Ski Resort? (1969–1975)

During this time, Mr. Donald S. Caplan made various attempts to establish a ski resort and other concessions within the park. He proposed building a ski lift at McAdams Peak but was turned down by William L. Rutherford, Director of the Department of Conservation. The Illinois Natural History Survey's wildlife specialist, Frank Bellrose, had noted two problems: first, it would disturb the wintering bald eagles, and, second, the Indian mounds and artifacts at the site were quite vulnerable.

Dr. Paul Kilburn, biology professor at nearby Principia College, suggested it would be ecologically less disruptive to place the ski lift in the east end of the park. By 1974, the ski lift was established, but operated for only a short time due to insufficient snow and the absence of a snow machine to lengthen the season.

Mr. Caplan complained that summer use was impossible at that site because people don't want to go to the top of the ski lift to be in the middle of a forest. In 1973, Caplan requested that he be able to hold six "contemporary" music concerts at the park. That was also turned down as inappropriate because there was no amphitheater. The whole enterprise faded away by 1975. In the years since then, the wooden ski facilities have been undergoing digestion by a grateful fungal world.

In 1985 the lodge was expanded to allow the facility to host larger gatherings and meetings. The expansion was done in a tasteful way that honors the distinct architecture of the original building.

More recently, the budget of the Department of Natural Resources has been shrinking, which has been problematic for maintaining the group camps. Fortunately, beginning in 2012, volunteers from the local Piasa Palisades Sierra Club group and the Godfrey-based Nature Institute have stepped forward to replace aging roofs and take care of other maintenance issues.

THE FIRST MUSEUM

For years the original visitor center was a small two-story log cabin on the north end of the present visitor center parking lot. That building has an interesting history. In the early 1930s the structure had been used as a corn storage barn as seen in a photograph from 1936. By 1940, big plans were underway to educate the public about the "veritable haven of nature lore in the bluff country of Pere Marquette region," reported a newspaper feature in May of that year. Under the leadership of Rev. George M. Link, the first park naturalist, the study of nature here was said to be attracting attention of people in all parts of the state. The log cabin became Link's Nature Center, where visitors were encouraged to visit and "prepare themselves in some measure for the glories of the park."

Current view of the former visitor center. Compare the landscape here with the historical view on p. 18.

A contemporary interior photograph shows that the nature center was lined floor to ceiling with more than 1000 volumes dealing with nature subjects. Numerous magazines and clippings were filed in this comprehensive nature library. In addition, there were many natural history artifacts on the shelves. Rev. Father Link kept weather records plus a year-by-year chart of the comings and goings of birds and the blooming dates of park wildflowers. A sign-in book was kept to record the numbers of park visitors each year. Each Saturday two guides were available to take visitors onto the park's trails. Visitors could change clothing and "pick up hiking equipment" in the room

Pioneer cabin. Present before park designation, this log structure was used as a corn crib in the 1930s. Later it was rehabbed as "Link's Nature Center," after the first park naturalist, Father George Link. Following that, it served as the visitor center before the present one was built nearby. Notice the essentially treeless prairie beyond the building. Since then, in the absence of fire, the slopes have become heavily wooded.

on the lower level. There were plans for the erection of five trailside museums that would deal with geology, archeology, botany, zoology, and ecology, respectively. The Pere Marquette Nature League had donated a barometer, and there were plans for donations of additional weather equipment.

From time to time through the 1980s, a park naturalist was stationed at the facility, but there was no museum or artifact collection. What became of those priceless original materials has not, in my search, come to light. For a time the cabin was used as the office of the park's site superintendent. In 1997, on the east side of the parking area, a beautiful new stone building opened, which functions today as headquarters and the visitor center.

Finally, we should note the contributions of farmer-entrepreneur Harry Hill Ferguson. In the 1920s he owned the 800-acre site centered in Camden Hollow on the east end of the park. Just west of Grafton, along Route 100, you can see his substantial stone building that presently houses the state's juvenile detention facility. In the 1930s he donated his property to the state, intending it to be an addition to the park.

Just beyond the hollow, along Route 100, is a cliff edge bearing a 7-foot carved dolomite cross, which is accessible from the highway via a set of stone steps. There is a parking area just beyond this prominence for those who would like to inspect this site. In the late 1920s, Mr. Ferguson engaged a skilled stone mason to build this cross and have it mounted in that location, where Père Marquette is said to have originally entered Illinois.

Aerial view of Ferguson Farm. Near the east end of the park, this site with its historic buildings currently houses a youth detention center.

On Sunday, September 1, 1929, two years before the park idea was conceived, the cross was dedicated and presented to the state by John D. McAdams and accepted by Governor Louis Emmerson. Clearly, preservation of this landscape was on the minds of these visionaries years before momentum grew that led to the establishment of this wonderful park.

CHAPTER 3

REGIONAL HUMAN HISTORY

THE SETTING

Even as Pleistocene ice sheets were retreating northward, this region became a major crossroads of human occupation. Archeological studies nearby, and throughout the Mississippi Valley, have documented that this region was rich in resources, an observation not lost on the human bands exploring this continent. The diverse ecology was due to the interface of prairies, upland forests, bottomland forests, and widespread wetlands. Plant and animal life was unusually diverse. In addition, it was the path of the rich Mississippi flyway for numerous species of migratory birds.

For humans, travel convenience in all directions was enhanced by the confluence of several larger and smaller rivers. The Native American groups described below would have been very familiar with this park's landscape and vicinity.

PREHISTORY: THE ECOLOGICAL CONTEXT

During the Late Pleistocene and Early Holocene, as the ice was disappearing from the Midwest, animal life was dominated in North America by large animals collectively called megafauna. These included such species as the wooly mammoth, mastodon, giant ground sloth, musk ox, giant beaver, a large armadillo, the dire wolf, saber-toothed cat, jaguar, horse, tapir, and the stag moose—more than 30 species altogether. In Illinois, there were few permanent Indian villages at that time. The hunters lived in temporary hunting camps as they followed their game resources.

For dating conventions I am using the following, scientifically neutral abbreviations in this guide. For distant times, BP means "years before present." For example, 7000 BP is equivalent to 5000 B.C. Dates for written history and times after the arrival of European humans in North America are labeled CE (common era), equivalent to A.D., and BCE (before the common era), equivalent to B.C.

The oldest of the local archeological findings, dating before 10,000 BP, is the Lincoln Hills site in Jersey County just north of this park. It was occupied by Clovis people, a group named for their characteristic tool styles, which were originally recovered at Clovis, New Mexico. Also known as Paleo hunters, they were attracted to this local site because of the availability of the chert required for tool making.

About 20 miles south of St. Louis is the Kimmswick site, now within Mastodon State Park. Occupied before 10,000 BP, it displays the largest Clovis artifact and bone deposit for this region. There are mastodon bones associated with stone tools, as well as the remains of peccary, sloth, carnivores, other ungulates, and muskrat. Also present were turtles, fish, birds, amphibians, squirrels, and various rodent species.

At the nearby Principia College campus along the bluffs at Elsah are mammoth remains, dated at 17,500 BP, which are currently being carefully excavated. Pollen analyses from these sites show that the tree flora was not spruce forest–dominated at this latitude. Instead the flora consisted of plant species more resembling our contemporary listing. In the case of mastodons, it demonstrates their capacity to adapt to ecologically different habitats. Paleo-Indians would certainly have regarded these animals as prime meat sources.

WHAT HAPPENED TO OUR MEGAFAUNA?

The short answer regarding the reasons for widespread megafauna extinction is that we remain uncertain and vigorous debate is ongoing. It seems that more genera of large animals were lost at the end of the Wisconsinan glacial epoch than during or between all the remaining previous ice ages (Reed, 1970). We do know that no animal species exceeding about 100 pounds survived in North America after that time.

The period of overlap of humans and megafauna is thought to be from 14,200 to 12,700 BP (Surovell & Grund, 2012). Some hold that these large species lasted until about 10,000 BP, although very little evidence of their existence, or that of the Paleo-Indian hunters, has been noted after 12,900 BP. The following are hypotheses now circulating.

1. Pleistocene overkill. Originated by Professor Paul Martin (1984) of the University of Arizona, this hypothesis holds that early man drove large animals to extinction by overhunting. It is argued that Clovis hunters were very efficient at the technology of killing large animals, and recent analysis indicates that this was their specialty. There is some evidence that Paleo-Indians were accompanied by domesticated dogs when they crossed the Bering land bridge after 13,500 BP, and that the hunters used dog packs during their hunts. Dogs would have been instrumental in making the hunters more effective in the pursuit of large game.

However, it seems doubtful to some scientists that there could have been enough hunters throughout the North American ranges of these animals to have brought about their almost simultaneous demise. It has been argued that humans were attracted to living in more temperate regions while megafauna occupied territories at higher latitudes. Also, according to scientists at the Illinois State Museum, only very few of the sites of megafauna remains are associated in any way with artifacts of early man.

Kolbert (2014) summarizes arguments that, before the arrival of humans, these animals had no experience avoiding efficient human-type predators. Also, crucial to the overkill argument is that many of the megafauna had long gestation times, leading to slow replacement rates.

2. Climate change. Critics of the overkill hypothesis hold that climate change strongly affected habitat. In many areas, a period of warming and drying followed the glacial retreat. Beginning abruptly, the Younger Dryas cooling period, named for an indicator plant in Europe, occurred between 12,800 BP and 11,600 BP. During this time the average temperature of the northern hemisphere dropped by 5°C–15°C.

On first consideration it would appear that climate change is insufficient, given that animals ought to be able to migrate to change their ranges and by the fact that many smaller animals did not face extinction. However, State Museum scientists analyzed genetic evidence and found that the larger animals actually did not migrate much. Therefore, they may have been quite stressed by climate change.

A recent study reported in 2014, led by researchers in Copenhagen, examined the 50,000-year history of vegetation and animal remains across the Siberian and North American Arctic. They studied the DNA of many large animals whose remains were preserved in permafrost. They found that these large animals depended on the high protein value of wildflowers that dominated arctic meadows. Later, climate-induced change to less nutritious grasses and shrubs may have greatly diminished the carrying capacity of these large, hungry mammals.

3. The bolide hypothesis, or "Clovis Comet hypothesis." This more recent finding resembles the now well-supported observations that explain the end of the Mesozoic and its fauna at 66 million BP. Related to the climate change idea above is some evidence that a bolide, probably a disintegrating comet, struck North America about 12,900 BP. In a number of North

American sites, this date is stratigraphically marked by a "black mat" of burned organic material plus minerals that indicate extraterrestrial impact.

The organic materials suggest widespread fires on the continent, which may explain the abrupt disappearance of large mammals and sharply diminished evidence of Clovis culture. Scientists have also found evidence of such an impact in Greenland ice strata, which forms layers that can be dated like tree rings. The impact marker includes unusual diamond dust of a structure that is not found on earth but is found in extraterrestrial bolides.

The resulting impact would have caused a multi-year darkening of the atmosphere that would have been accompanied by a substantial drop in annual temperatures. No large crater has been found, but it may have been cushioned by the contemporary Laurentide ice cap. Some think that such an impact may have triggered the onset of the Younger Dryas period mentioned earlier.

4. Disease. Some pathogens carried by people and perhaps their dogs may have jumped species barriers. The study indicated, for example, that canine distemper carried by Indian dog packs can be lethal when jumping to different species. But could species-jumping diseases account for such widespread extinctions among different animal families?

5. Pace of ecological change. Recent studies of animal DNA, and what has been called "niche conservatism," suggest a lack of sufficient capacity to adapt. An ecological niche, also called "ecospace," is defined as the total impact of an organism in an area: its food habits, interactions with other species, and all physical aspects of its environment. The post-Pleistocene (Holocene) period was noteworthy for significant fluctuations in mean temperatures and precipitation patterns. Species react variously to changes in their ecospace.

Scientists continue to probe deeper into the many changes that took place on this continent after the end of Wisconsinan glaciation. Finally, and my own opinion, it's quite possible that there was a "cascade of events"—no one single cause, but stress from different angles. As ongoing studies are reported, we will doubtlessly come to know much more about what happened to megafauna and to Clovis culture.

REGIONAL ARCHEOLOGY

Moving up in time, we are fortunate to have the Koster site in nearby Greene County, which is renowned in archeological circles for having documented a deep and nearly continuous prehistory of the Illinois and Mississippi Valleys. Between 1969 and 1978, the site on Theodore and Mary Koster's farm was excavated by a team led originally by Professor Stuart Struever of

Northwestern University. As the site's importance became clear, the Center for American Archeology (CAA) was established at Kampsville in Calhoun County. One can visit its small museum there.

The CAA's investigations recorded an almost unbroken sequence of around 300 generations of occupancy, in 26 occupation levels (8400–800 BP). Major villages appeared at the earliest period, as well as 7000 and 5300 BP. The earliest occupation levels were about 30 feet below the present ground level. Gradual deposition of sediments from upland erosion made this site ideal for preserving continuous history.

There were no monuments or major earthworks nearby, but investigators have documented, regionally, the existence of thousands of smaller mounds and occupation sites. The analysis of such a large quantity of artifacts and natural materials has given us an unparalleled view of social evolution from early camp and village life through ever-advancing technology, population growth, social complexity, and food sources that evolved with passing time.

Pere Marquette State Park is also within the region centered on Cahokia Mounds, about 40 miles to the southeast. That World Heritage Site has been the focus of extensive archeological investigations, especially covering Mississippian culture. With those studies, plus many from other regional sites, we can piece together a fascinating picture of the evolving stages of American Indian life during the Holocene. We can assume that all of the cultures described below would have been familiar with the unusual topography of this park and its rich surrounding resources.

HISTORY OF HUMAN OCCUPATION

For the sequence of cultures summarized below, the dates vary depending on specific regions of eastern North America. Here I am following Iseminger's (2010) summary of occupancy dates for Cahokia Mounds, which is the closest major site.

PALEO-INDIANS (11,500–10,000 BP)

Small bands of hunters, also called Clovis hunters, lived in Illinois as early as 12,000 BP, a time when conifer forests were replacing glacial tundra. Mastodons, giant ground sloths, and deer roamed the landscape.

The people's tools included distinctive stone points and scrapers that have been found at such kill sites as Kimmswick, south of St. Louis. Because their favored prey species were on the move, populations were sparse and their camps temporary. Stone points were usually knapped from non-local sources of rock, implying that they traveled hundreds of miles per year to hunt and retool. Well-made projectile points of this period are found widely in the Midwest landscape.

Around 9000 BP, later Paleo-Indians, called the Dalton culture, adapted to a moderated climate where deciduous forests were replacing the cold-climate conifer ecology. They settled in the Mississippi Valley in larger numbers, developed formal cemeteries, and met for ritualized exchange. Because of expanding woodlands, climate shift, and large mammal extinctions, they developed a foraging lifestyle.

ARCHAIC (10,000–2600 BP)

Temperatures of this post-glacial landscape continued to moderate during this long period. Because some large animal species were hunted to extinction, animals new to Illinois, including white-tailed deer, raccoon, and opossum, became common, along with other mammals and birds we would recognize. From the thousands of Archaic sites that have been found in Illinois, we know this culture flourished. Sites range from temporary camps to permanent villages. The people's more variable tools were made from local sources, including bone and mussel shell. Wooden artifacts, in the form of charcoal, are occasionally found among other remains.

Divisible into Early, Middle, and Late periods, Archaic peoples transitioned from nomadic hunters and fisherfolk to a more sedentary lifestyle. The finding of heavy stone manos, metates, and pestles used for grinding seeds are evidence of permanent village life. Their diet included a wide variety of animal and plant materials. By 7000 BP, gourds and squash appear in the archeological record as well as seeds from many other species.

As warmer and drier conditions developed in the Midwest, prairie vegetation began as far east as Ohio. Called the Hypsithermal climatic interval, this was a time when people made more use of the river valleys and less of uplands. At the Koster site, structures requiring large support posts were built; there was also a cemetery for this permanent settlement. By 5000 BP, temperatures and precipitation were close to today's levels. Deciduous forests followed river valleys, but on the uplands, forests were replaced by prairies.

In the late Archaic, around 4000 BP, recovered materials show that larger sedentary populations engaged in trade ranging from the Gulf Coast to Lake Superior. Seed and nut collecting and animal hunting began to be supplemented by agriculture. Native species cultivated for the first time included several oil- or starch-bearing seeds. The people cultivated sumpweed (*Iva annua*), sunflower (*Helianthus annuus*), goosefoot (*Chenopodium* spp.), knotweed (*Polygonum erectum*), maygrass (*Phalaris caroliniana*), little barley (*Hordeum pusillim*), and squash (*Cucurbita pepo*).

Close to the end of the Archaic, archeologists discovered burials of high-status individuals, especially in the "Red Ocher mortuary complex" (3500–2500 BP). By grinding the brick-red hematite rock, people produced red ocher dust that was sprinkled over human remains. There is evidence the Archaic people lived in temporary housing. Their distinctive, large leaf-shaped projectile points, polished stone celts, banner stones, gorgets, and copper ornaments demonstrated their high level of craftsmanship.

In summary, the Archaic period was a 7000-year span of continuous trends in population size, inventiveness, exploitation of resources, and social organization, and noteworthy for adding plant cultivation to hunting and gathering.

WOODLAND (2600–1250 BP)

The Woodland period, divided among Early, Middle, and Late phases, ended just before historical contact with European travelers.

Early Woodland (2600–2150 BP)

The period is marked by the disappearance of Late Archaic and Red Ocher cultures. This is also the beginning of pot-making and the first handmade pottery found in Illinois.

Middle Woodland (2150–1700 BP)

Named for an Ohio site, Hopewellian people spread widely from Ohio, occupying the lower Illinois Valley by about 2000 BP. They were noted for their mound building and bluff-top cemeteries. Eventually there were over 350 settlements and more than 300 mound groups in the floodplains and adjacent bluff-top cemeteries. Throughout the Upper Mississippi Valley there are thousands of bluff-top burial mounds, including (conservatively) at least 40 within Pere Marquette State Park.

The high point of the park is called Tucker Knob. It is a large Indian mound at the junction of the Hickory Trail North.

McAdams Peak shelter. Built by the Civilian Conservation Corps, it honors William McAdams who did early archeological work in the area.

The Middle Woodland people's cultivation of a number of seed plants that yielded starch and oils gave them generally good nutrition. Recovered from their sites were evidence of nuts, knotweed, goosefoot, marsh elder, sunflower, squash, gourds, and barley. Tobacco (*Nicotiana* sp.) also appears. Corn, also called maize (*Zea mays*), was introduced from Mexico into the American Southwest about 4100 BP. A relative latecomer here, it became more widely planted after 1500–1600 BP. Archeological findings show that communication and trade were widespread, virtually continental in scope, and rituals guided most aspects of life.

Late Woodland (1700–1250 BP)

Studies show that, by now, maize had become an important food crop. Its capacity for surplus production led to the development of larger and more concentrated populations. In turn, social and political complexity emerged. Prior to this time no excess population pressure had been put on the resource base.

Emergent Mississippian (750–1050 CE)

After Late Woodland, a transition to the next phase saw these trends continue. Maize culture was intensified after 800 CE, forming a Mississippi basin corn region ranging from Ohio to the plains of northern Tennessee. In the Cahokia region, whose radius includes the Pere Marquette park vicinity, plant and pollen remains indicate clearance and development of agricultural fields. However, by this time no sudden effect on political organization is detected.

Mississippian (1050–1400 CE)

As exemplified by village states such as Cahokia, by Mississippian times trade and social organization had reached their climax. Considered a kingdom by some archeologists, the Mississippian people were known for building huge mounds. They also built neighborhoods surrounding courtyards and plazas. This potential had been realized by the food surpluses from efficient agricultural production. The cultivation of maize, squash, and beans, often called a "triad," emerged from Mexico. It provided a calorie-rich and balanced diet. This agriculture, plus enhanced distant trade, spread widely throughout the Midwest and Southeast.

Residents were also skilled makers of small, finely chipped arrowheads, polished stone celts, and chunky stones. Many kinds of implements and ornaments were fashioned of bone, shell, copper, and clay. The Mississippian people smoked equal-armed pipes and made flat-bottomed ceramic vessels with handles in a variety of shapes and wares.*

An always intriguing question is what caused the abandonment of an apparently thriving culture. It was probably a combination of stresses. During the community's maximum development, greatly increased population pressure placed strain on regional wood and thatch supplies. The increasing scarcity of these construction materials, plus firewood, medicinals, and animals, is believed to have contributed to the abandonment of these population centers by 1300 CE. Lopinot and Woods (1993) hypothesized that overexploitation of wood may have led to regional erosion and a ruined agricultural system. Toward the end, the need to use trees to build stockades suggests serious regional conflict. Recent evidence suggests that a major flood in 1200 CE inundated the entire American Bottoms region. Finally, the advent of the medieval warm period may have been an influence, but regardless, a region-wide "vacant quarter" occurred that lasted from the 14th to the 16th centuries.

Late Prehistoric (1250–1650 CE)

This era saw the emergence of the historic tribes of the Illiniwek Confederacy, which came to be called the Illinois by the French. These tribes, about 10 groups from the Algonquian language family, lived in bark-sided huts, raised maize, and hunted bison on the prairies with stone-tipped arrows. Some anthropologists suggest that descendants of Cahokian culture did not lead to the Illiniwek group but may be more closely related to the Siouan-speaking tribes to the west. This remains uncertain at present.

---

*We are fortunate to have the nearby Cahokia Mounds State Historic Site, which features an excellent interpretive museum.

NATIVE AMERICANS IN EARLY HISTORIC TIMES

Considering northeastern North America as a whole, anthropologists estimate that before European contact, Native Americans numbered between 2 million and 10 million. By 1890, their populations had been reduced to perhaps 250,000.

At the time of first European contact, Native Americans of Illinois consisted of loosely confederated bands variously called Hileni, Illiniwek, Illini, or Illinois by the French. The term "Illinois" translates as "man" or "human being." The 10 groups, in rough order of decreasing size, were the Peoria, Kaskaskia, Cahokia, Tamaroa, Moingwena, Taponero, Coiracoentanon, Chaokia, Chipussea, and Michigamea. With respect to Illinois, the reasons for their decline are detailed below.

From the early historic period, what we know of Indian cultures within Illinois was only occasionally recorded by European travelers as they encountered them. From these records we learn that, by the 17th and early 18th centuries, and perhaps earlier, the Illiniwek tribes faced conflict with the fiercer and more numerous Iroquois warriors to the east. As first reported by LaSalle in 1680, the Illiniwek suffered disastrous and repeated raids at the hands of the Iroquois. In 1736, a French government census counted only about 600 warriors, a greatly reduced population.

In western Illinois there were few Indians remaining when the first settlers arrived. From the Smithsonian's *Handbook of American Indians* (Hodge, 1907, 1910) we learn that the remnants of the once great Sauk, Fox, Potawatomie, and Kickapoo tribes were subjected to numerous "treaties" between 1789 and 1867. Each "agreement" constricted territory and moved the tribes westward, essentially out of the way of European settlement. By 1846 the last of the organized tribes had moved west of the Mississippi, occupying several temporary locations, eventually ending up in "Indian Territory," now Oklahoma.

The culture of Illinois Indians was a mixture of Eastern Woodlands–Eastern Plains, a reflection of the ecological transition between woodlands and prairies where they lived. Illinois Indians may have arrived in the state as early as 1500 BP. Members of all groups spoke Algonquian language dialects that were mostly mutually intelligible to their neighbors of that language family. This linguistic group was the largest in North America and occupied about a quarter of the continent's native populations. Modern DNA studies (Shook & Smith, 2008) indicate that Illinoian bands evolved from proto-Algonquian peoples who were in the Northeast at least as early as 3000 BP.

Algonquian-speaking neighbors to the north were Potawatomi and Miami; to the south, Chickasaw and Shawnee. To the west were the Siouan-speaking Kansa (Kaw) and Osage. Immediate eastern neighbors at the time were undocumented, although the reported aggression by Iroquois arriving from the east probably answers that question.

The semi-permanent villages occupied by the Illinoian bands were concentrated along the Illinois and Mississippi Rivers, from the mouth of the Missouri, Illinois, and Kaskaskia Rivers, northward to the vicinity of present-day Starved Rock State Park. In those days rivers and adjacent backwaters and sloughs were extraordinary resources for obtaining animal protein and useful plants. Larger game could also be obtained not far inland.

A Tragic Decline

Beginning about 1666, the locations of villages underwent a series of changes directly related to the availability of trade goods. Tribal members were quickly attracted to the higher technology of steel blades, and later, guns, among many other items. In that year about 80 Illinois Indians visited the Jesuit mission at Chequamegon on the south shore of Lake Superior. In the 1680s Fort Saint Louis was established by La Salle and Tonty at Starved Rock, opposite Kaskaskia village. Many Indian groups came to live in the neighborhood to engage in trade. By 1700 trade goods could no longer be carried from Canada to Illinois country, but were instead moved upriver from Louisiana.

In 1673 the best-documented population estimate of Illinois Indians was approximately 10,000. By 1700, after 30 years of intensive white contact, the total population was closer to 5800. By 1736, the estimate was 2500 persons. At the end of the Revolutionary War era, in 1800, the 700 persons remaining on the east side of the Mississippi River were reduced to about 500.

In a series of treaties beginning in 1803, the Indians ceded all claims to land within present-day Illinois. By 1814, General William Henry Harrison, newly appointed governor of Indiana Territory, noted that these once populous Illinois tribes were reduced to about 30 warriors. In 1832 the remaining Illini groups were moved to a reservation in eastern Kansas. By 1873, after more moves, the population remnants were finally located in northeast Indian Territory, later becoming Oklahoma. By 1950, 439 Peorias were counted and 323 Miamis. It is doubtful that any full-blooded Illinoian Indians still survive.

Reasons for the Decline

After Euro-American contact, the reasons for population decline are multiple:

1. Intertribal raids. Ongoing hostilities, including slave acquisition, were fairly constant. Later, some skirmishes were instigated by colonial and American powers that enlisted warriors as allies.

2. Christianity and monogamy. Traditionally, high death rates had been countered by the polygamy practiced by tribal males. The resulting accelerated birth rate kept population sizes fairly constant. For this reason it has been estimated that polygamy has been common in 85% of traditional cultures worldwide. Among local tribes, acceptance of Catholicism, and therefore monogamy, greatly decreased replacement rates.

3. Disease. Tribal members had little immune protection against European diseases such as smallpox, measles, malaria, and gonorrhea. Smallpox episodes decimated some villages by 50%. Gonorrhea, carried by traders, soldiers, and later, colonists, effectively sterilized numerous tribal women.

4. Alcohol. Until the second quarter of the 18th century there was no excessive liquor consumption, as it was restricted in trade through Canada. By 1750, when most trade came through Louisiana, the French persisted in supplying brandy to the Indians. Alcohol abuse and addiction greatly increased violence among tribal members and between tribes. Worse, during the summers they neglected to trade for clothes or put up winter supplies. As the inevitable cold descended, numerous Indian families starved or froze to death.

As pointed out by Blasingham (1956), native bands are "tradition-directed" societies where social order is relatively stable through the generations. But their traditions could not withstand the changes resulting from increasing contact with white hunters, soldiers, traders, and farmers. They were unable to adapt to this accelerating disruption of their traditional lives. By the latter 1800s, the Illini became quite dispirited as their centuries-old lifestyles were destroyed.

THE FRENCH PERIOD (1663–1775)

On May 17, 1673, a decade after Louis XIV created the crown colony of New France in 1663, the first official expedition set off to explore the "Grande Rivieure" the Indians said was to the west. The King's Minister in Paris had stated that a principal goal was to discover a passage to the South Sea, later renamed the Pacific Ocean. More than a century earlier the lower Mississippi had been extensively explored by Hernando de Soto. Until he died of fever in 1542, de Soto's expedition traveled land and waters well into Arkansas. But even 130 years later, connections to rivers farther north remained uncertain.

Leaving the Mission of St. Ignace in the Mackinac Straits between Lower Michigan and the Upper Peninsula, the government expedition set out for Green Bay in two bark canoes. The group of seven was commanded by Sueur Louis Jolliet, a young trader and explorer, and accompanied by Père Jacques Marquette, a Jesuit chaplain, and five others. From there they proceeded up the Fox River and over a portage to the Wisconsin River. Henceforth they were in terra incognita.

They entered the Mississippi River on June 17 of that year and encountered Illinois Indians near present-day Keokuk, Iowa. There they received a calumet, a peace pipe, to safeguard their trip. This "passport" was helpful for several hundred miles as they floated southward.

Sometime during the summer of 1673, these first Europeans found the bluffs between Grafton and Alton quite awe-inspiring. They were also the first white men to see the ancient pictographs east of the mouth of Piasa Creek. At that latitude and time, Joliet and Marquette found a densely settled region, fully utilized by Native Americans of the Illinois confederacy. As agriculturalists, they cultivated corn, beans, and squash above the prominent bluffs. Referring to the high bluffs near present-day Alton, Marquette wrote:

> "We saw upon one of them two painted monsters which at first made us afraid, and upon which the boldest savages dare not long rest their eyes. They were as large as a calf, they have horns on their heads like those of deer, a horrible look, red eyes, a beard like a tiger's, a face somewhat like a man's, a body covered with scales, and so long a tail that it winds all around the body, passing above the head and going back between the legs, ending in a fish's tail. Green, red and black are the three colors composing the picture. Moreover, these two monsters are so well painted that we cannot believe that any savage is their author; for good painters in France would find it difficult to paint as well, and besides, they are so high up on the rock that it is difficult to reach that place conveniently to paint them" (Thwaites, 1900; Kellogg, 1917).

This is the first written record of what is now locally referred to as the Piasa Bird. Sadly, in the mid-1850s, the rock face bearing the Piasa Bird was quarried away for lime.

In July, Joliet and Marquette's party continued down the Mississippi to the Arkansas River, where they decided that the Mississippi emptied into the Gulf of Mexico. Wisely, the expedition leaders chose not to continue southward as the Indians of the region were hostile and had Spanish trade merchandise. The leaders assumed they might be in danger of being captured by the Spanish.

Reversing course, Joliet and Marquette ascended the Mississippi and entered the "River of the Illinois," according to Marquette, having learned from the Indians that it was a shortcut to the Lake of the Illinois (Lake

Michigan). Thus in September 1673, we have the first known entry of white men into Illinois. Immediately to their right was a view of this future park. Just north of Grafton, a commemorative cross hewn of native stone now stands along the highway at the edge of the bluff, at what was once the mouth of the Illinois River, and which is now within Pere Marquette State Park. The explorers were impressed by the soil fertility and abundance of wildlife as they paddled northward toward present-day Chicago.

The expedition's favorable report on the Illinois Valley made it of major future importance. In the next 50 years, there was much travel over these rivers, especially for beaver trade. But for various reasons, including the presence of malaria, there was little settlement.

THE BRITISH PERIOD (1763–1776)

On February 10, 1763, a century after the first exploration, all of New France east of the Mississippi River (except Louisiana) was ceded to the British. This led to a more turbulent period. British occupation of the forts to the north and east was rapid. Chief Pontiac of the Ottawas attacked the British, taking all forts but Pitt, Niagara, and Detroit. A year later, in 1764, St. Louis was founded downstream, across the river.

At Kaskaskia in 1773 the Illinois Land Company, represented by William Murray, purchased two huge tracts from the Indians. One tract, which included the land of Pere Marquette State Park, began at the mouth of the Missouri River and proceeded up the Illinois and Mississippi Rivers to the Chicago River. In those days such a tract could be had for five shillings, some cloth, livestock, and ammunition.

Still, exactly what belonged to whom was vague. In 1775 the region as far south as the Ohio River became a part of Quebec Province. After the Boston Tea Party, the colonists also let it be known that they were not in accord with the Quebec Act on religious and expansionist grounds. Illinois country was claimed by several states, and many persons were stockholders in land companies.

THE AMERICAN PERIOD (AFTER 1776)

TRAVELERS AND EXPLORERS

Travel, especially by river, became more frequent. Not long after Jefferson organized the purchase of Louisiana Territory, Lewis and Clark entered the Missouri River in 1803. Later, in August of 1806, Lt. Zebulon Pike's expedition passed the mouth of Illinois River on his search for the source of the Mississippi.

Across the Mississippi, just west of the future Alton, was the east end of a trail called Portage des Sioux. This important 2-mile-long cutoff saved 20 miles of river travel for Indians between the Missouri and the Upper Mississippi and Illinois Rivers. In legend the Sioux once escaped from enemies in hot pursuit using this route. In 1799, a village on the Mississippi shore by this name grew up around a Spanish fort, which later became a French settlement just before the Louisiana Purchase.

In July 1810 there occurred a noteworthy series of raids by Indians of the Illinois Territory against citizens of the Louisiana Territory. Sac warriors stole horses and goods, with the ensuing pursuit ending in loss of Indian lives. During the War of 1812, Portage des Sioux was a military operations center against Indians of upper Louisiana, but it gradually fell into decline. In due course, in July 1815, 37 tribes and the governors of Illinois and Missouri signed the treaty at Portage des Sioux.

Timothy Flint, a Presbyterian and sometime Congregational pastor, was rare among early adventurers as the keeper of a journal. He traveled in this region around 1815–1816, at a time when St. Louis had about 2000 residents. He reported that the Illinois River, just above its confluence with the Mississippi, was a "clear and broad stream four hundred and fifty yards wide in a channel as straight and regular as a canal." Not far above the mouth a prairie skirted the river. "It is beautiful, being from two to three miles in width... Beyond this prairie is a short open woods, and the whole is bounded by a lime-stone bluff, smooth and perpendicular, and generally from two to three hundred feet high" (Flint [1918] 1968).

On the west side, Flint recorded the presence of some War of 1812 veterans who had come to the "bounty lands" to examine the value of their tracts. Along the river Flint encountered families of Potawatomie Indians and mixed-blood French, living in wretched conditions.

Settlement of the Region

That same year, John Messenger, Surveyor-General of Illinois Territory, plus two deputy surveyors and four chain carriers, began surveying a meridian from the south bank of the Illinois River, eventually proceeding north through Graham Hollow, over intervening ridges and prairies to Beardstown in 15 days. This is now a township line, crossing Route 100 just to the east of the Pere Marquette main campground entrance road.

The last Native Americans to claim land in the region were the Kickapoo tribe. In July 1819, the prairie country east and north of the mouth of the

Illinois River was purchased from them by Auguste Chouteau and Col. Benjamin Stephenson of Edwardsville, acting for the United States.*

The territory containing Grafton and Pere Marquette State Park was designated as Grafton Township in 1878 and later changed to Quarry Township in 1880. The township was first settled by five veterans of the regular Army, who arrived in 1819. Gilbert Lake commemorates David Gilbert, who arrived during this time and settled on the shore of that body of water.

In 1821, seven new counties were created south and east of the Illinois River. In the same year George Finney, one of the veterans, and John Evans entered land near the mouth of the Illinois River, becoming the first settlers in what is now Pere Marquette State Park.

Economic Growth

By the 1830s the region saw considerable activity. Finney, in 1832, platted the village of Camden in what is now called Camden Hollow. The site was on the Mississippi River at the mouth of the Illinois River and was said at that time to have significant growth potential.

In 1830 James Mason chose a suitable location to establish a ferry over the Mississippi and Missouri Rivers, with the intent to build a road to the new settlement. He settled just east of Camden Hollow and in 1833 built the first home in what became Grafton. During this same time, the Erie Canal opened and Chicago was platted. In the spring of 1831, young Abe Lincoln helped build a flat boat along the Sangamon River, which he and two others navigated past Grafton and the future park on their float to New Orleans. In March 1832, the "upper cabin cruiser," *Talisman*, from Cincinnati, Ohio, passed the future Pere Marquette State Park, continuing up the ice-choked Illinois River bound for Springfield.

By 1836 the future Grafton was surveyed, and a planked earth wharf called Mason's Landing was built. Lots sold for $400 to $1500 and the town soon boomed. Permanent settlers seized opportunities to open several stores and warehouses, a sawmill, blacksmith shop, hotel, and more residences. William Williams and James Tucker settled in hollows that today bear their names.

Where the park lodge now stands, the town of Hartford was platted in the fall of 1837. Later its 40 blocks were twice sold for taxes when Illinois was in the throes of a financial panic. The sole reminders of the hoped-for town are the graveyard and little white church bearing this name, at the west end

---

*Col. Stephenson's Edwardsville home, built in 1820, is now a fully restored historical museum.

of the campground. That same year, in nearby fast-growing Alton, newspaper publisher Elijah Lovejoy was shot, thus becoming a martyr of the abolitionists.

In 1844 the worst flood of the 19th century inundated the new town, which must have dampened some enthusiasm but apparently not for long. During the 1850s, Mason's Landing became a wood and coal center for river traffic where corded wood from surrounding forests was floated in boats to St. Louis. Riverboats had a voracious appetite for cordwood, which led inevitably to deforestation of the bottomlands and any uplands where wood could be moved to a boat landing. It wasn't until later in the 20th century that flooding became more common as a result of levees that constricted river flow during high water.

Coal appeared and became a fuel used on Mississippi River steamboats that plied the river all the way to St. Paul. On the Illinois River one could transfer to canal boats for Chicago and east. Large rafts of pine logs and lumber from Wisconsin floated to Grafton and were taken south. Through the decades increasing numbers of immigrants moved up these rivers in search of lands to settle. As the 19th century progressed, commerce increased along with more frequent ferry boat trips. In 1852 an Alton–Springfield rail route was open for business, which provided even more choice of goods.

In 1857, quarrying began and a steam ferry operated at Mason's Landing. Building stone was cut there using a work force of up to 2000 men. Stone was shipped on barges to St. Louis and also placed along the river to control the channel. Piers of the Meredosia and Hannibal Railroad bridges are made of Grafton stone of this era. The quarrying in nearby Alton that destroyed the Piasa Bird dates from this era.

ORIGIN OF THE HARTFORD CHURCH

From 1857 to the present, the Grafton Methodist congregation has occupied a church that replaced an earlier building dating from 1837. In the 1870s their pastor, Henry Delicate, became aware that a group of families in Hartford, formerly Criswell's Point, was holding services in homes of congregation members. Henry decided they needed a church, and he saw that one got built at his personal expense.

Traveling to Alton, he obtained the necessary lumber and had it shipped up river by the *Calhoun*, a boat built in 1876 in Jeffersonville, Indiana. It was a wood-hulled, side-wheel packet boat, and this must have been one of the first such trips up the Mississippi and Illinois Rivers. When the captain learned the lumber was for a church, he donated the cost of shipment and helped unload it at Hartford Landing.

In August 1876, the church was being built at the apparently preexisting Hartford graveyard. As reported in the *Grafton Weekly Republican* (August 1876): "Our pastor Delicate is taking it very much to heart that his congregations are so small and those of his nearest neighbors, the saloon keepers, are so large, and what they keep on hand warms more than his sermons do." Pastor Delicate divided his time between the two congregations. That year he was appointed to serve a second year in Grafton. During his pastorate there he reorganized the Sunday school and baptized 56 adults and 20 children. Along Route 100, on the west boundary of the

Hartford Church. This picturesque historic building is seen from the highway between the campground and the main lodge area.

park campground, the little white Hartford Church remains. The building, with its graveyard, is now surrounded by the park.*

As the Civil War approached, an underground railroad operated successfully with the dedication of Grafton residents. Escaped slaves were met at Calhoun Point and sent to Otterville, Princeton, and on to Canada and freedom. During the Civil War there was a loss of communications and ferry travel ceased.

Quarrying remained a major industry until the 1970s and 1980s, when the remaining quarries were closed. Tourism and commercial travel were given a real boost when a road was constructed along the bluffs between Grafton and Alton in the late 1920s. Originally named in honor of John McAdams, the road was improved later and became known as the Great River Road. Now in various forms, the route by that name runs along the Mississippi for 3000 miles, from Minnesota to the Gulf of Mexico. Along this lengthy route Pere Marquette State Park has to be on the short list of the most beautiful and significant attractions.

---

*These notes and reminiscences were provided by my friend Scott Delicate, great-grandson of Pastor Henry Delicate. Also included are notes from Mrs. Marjorie Dintelmann, whose grandfather helped build the church.

CHAPTER 4

GEOGRAPHY, ECOLOGY, AND CLIMATE

PHYSICAL STATUS

SIZE OF THE PARK

Early in the Great Depression, about 1500 acres were included in the originally purchased parklands. Since then, additional tracts have been offered and purchased. A large contribution, the St. Andrew ridge on the north end, was donated by the National Park Service. These additions have brought the current acreage to approximately 8050, making Pere Marquette Illinois' largest state park that has no mining history.

PLACE IN MIDWESTERN GEOGRAPHY

In classifications of regional biogeography, the park is placed near the southwestern boundary of the Till Plains section, of the Central Lowlands Province, within the Lincoln Hills and Salem Plateau sections of the Ozark Plateaus to the west.

A section of the Illinois state map that shows forest cover for the park region.

The park area itself, and adjacent Calhoun County, were not directly covered by glacial ice. For this latitude of Illinois, the topography is rugged. Numerous outcrops of dolomite, limestone, and shale are exposed on cliffs and steep slopes.

Specifically, for Illinois geography, we have Schwegman's (1973) classification that places the park entirely within the Driftless Section of the Middle Mississippi Border Division. This emphasizes the finding that the park acreage was never under Pleistocene ice. However, the Pleistocene epoch did leave a widespread and conspicuous legacy in the form of deep deposits of wind-borne soil particles, called loess. These deposits form a mantle 50–100 feet thick covering the underlying bedrock.

A look at the map of the park shows an L-shaped tract that corresponds with a sharp bend in the Illinois River and the nearby Mississippi River. The reasons for this "notch" in the otherwise arrowhead-shaped outline of Illinois will be considered in the geology discussion (Chapter 5).

Climatic Basis of Life

A region's climate is certainly the crucial factor in determining what species can survive or thrive, and the extremes are much more important than the averages. Here, our continental climate is noted for hot summers and cold winters, and an annual temperature range of greater than 100°F is not uncommon.

Local Statistics

The heat record is 112°F for July 14 and 15, 1954, and the cold record is –15°F on January 11, 1962. The coldest month is usually January, and the hottest is usually August. The frost-free growing season is about 200 days, with the first frost arriving in late October and the last frost in early to mid-April.

Precipitation averages 35 to 40 inches, roughly evenly distributed, or with more in spring and early summer. Strong winds and hail can accompany storms more than once a year. In an average year the skies are cloudy 40% of the time, partly cloudy 30%, and clear 30%. Possible sunshine averages 70% in summer months and 45% in December through February.

Prevailing winds are from the south and southwest May through November, but in other months can be from the north and northeast. Highest average wind velocity is usually from March through April at 11 mph. Lowest wind velocity occurs July through August at 7 mph.

Remember that averages are only part of the story. Periodic droughts or wet spells occur unpredictably in any season and may alternate unevenly within any given decade. Every few years, extreme weather events such as searing heat, ice storms, large hail, or damaging high winds may occur randomly. In the end, the resulting flora is composed of species that can survive these stresses. Here, I refer mainly to flora rather than fauna, because plants are the base of the food chain. Survival of animals anywhere is determined initially by the nature of existing vegetation cover.

Stelle (1993) has pointed out that Illinois lies at the eastern vertex of a triangle of cool and dry continental air extending eastward from the Rocky Mountains. The northern edge is defined by the average January storm path with its zone of heavy snowfall to the north. The southern boundary is the average winter Gulf Coast storm track noted for its characteristic heavy winter rains. Jet stream–based northward or southward fluctuation of these paths can explain the unusual year-to-year climatic variation at this point in North America.

Topography

If we consider the lowest regional base level to be the Mississippi and Illinois river pools as impounded by Lock and Dam 26 at Alton, we have a figure of 419 feet above sea level. The park's high point, Tucker Knob, an Indian mound built of loess (see p. 26), has an elevation of 892 feet. This yields a total relief of 473 feet.

Within the park, most ridge tops measure approximately 815 feet in elevation, with the ravine bottoms at about 500 feet, thus yielding an average relief of about 315 feet. This is still considerable for a state whose landscape was otherwise mostly flattened by glacial ice. Much of Illinois looked like this park, or the central Ozarks, before Pleistocene glaciations.

Soils

Soils are not easily identified without some specialized tools and instruments. Below, at the risk of oversimplifying, I will attempt a summary for the park. Soils are grouped according to parent material, surface color, degree of subsoil development, and natural soil drainage. Using soil core samplers, the depth of three "horizons" are normally measured: "A horizon" is the topsoil, a mix of mineral particles, roots, and decomposed organic matter; "B horizon" is the subsoil, with less organic matter; and "C horizon" is unaltered or slightly altered parent material.

A loess bank along an old pioneer road section of the Hickory Trail South. Exposed roots of the tree base show the rate of erosion during its lifetime.

In soil studies, the site's slope is also noted because it relates to erosion potential and the types of vegetation that can survive. The following letters may be added to a description: A = < 2% slope, B = 2%–4% slope, C = 4%–7% slope, D = 7%–12% slope, E = 12%–18% slope, F = 18%–30% slope, and G = > 30% slope.

In the surrounding region, bluff-top soils are of the general prairie type, known as the Hamburg silt, which is normally grass covered rather than forested. The parent material is unaltered loess, a glacial silt of wind-blown origin. The upper horizon is very friable, grayish-brown to brown in color.

Below the loess layer, the regional underlying bedrock soil particle source is calcareous. This means it is mostly calcium carbonate of ancient marine origin. The following three soil groups are found in the park as sampled from the St. Andrew ridge area, the northern portion of the park.

Sylvan-Bold Complex

This type is found in the western and southwestern parts of the county on deep deposits of loess, and where topography is steep or moderately sloping. Acidity ranges from slightly acid to slightly alkaline, at pH 6.3–8. Sylvan is calcareous throughout. Profile (horizon) depths are: A = 0.8 inch, B = 6–8 inches, and C = 36–60+ inches. Bold is light-colored (yellowish) spots on eroded ridges. On steeper slopes, natural erosion has been severe enough to keep soil development to a minimum. Profile depths are A = 0–6 inches and C = 6–40+ inches.

Fayette Silt Loam

Well drained and light colored, this soil type is developed from loess under forest vegetation. It occurs on slopes from gentle to very steep sites. It is slightly acidic with a pH 5.4–6.5. Profile depths are: A = 0–14 inches, B = 14–59 inches, and C = 59+ inches.

Elsah Cherty Silt Loam

Light-colored and moderately to well-drained, this silty bottomland soil contains fragments of chert. It is restricted to bottomlands and valley walls in unglaciated southwestern Jersey County. It is formed from the weathering of cherty limestone and is slightly acidic to neutral, at pH 6.5–7. Profile depths are: A = 0–15 inches and C = 15–50+ inches.

PLANTS AND ANIMALS

Vegetation Types

Names given to regional vegetation are usually based on communities of dominant genera or species. These serve as indicators of habitat types and climate tolerance. Original field notes taken during the land survey of March 29, 1819, listed specimens of the same species that occur here today. Those surveyors considered the park area as "unfit for cultivation" due to rocks, topography, and thin soil. The understory along section lines was said to consist of "vines, briars, and sassafras."

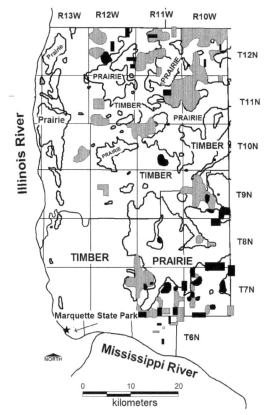

Map of Jersey County (lower half) and Green County, based on observations by general land office surveyors in the early 19th century. These first records documented the vegetation pattern here before the advent of agriculture. Much of the landscape north and east of the park was called barrens. These were islands of scattered, often stunted trees interspersed within a continuous prairie. In prehistory, such a landscape was maintained by frequent fires. Gray shapes indicate barrens, and black areas are thinly timbered sites. Reproduced by permission from Kilburn et al. (2009).

The study by Kilburn et al. (2009) analyzed surveyors' records of public domain lands made before 1820 by the General Land Office (GLO). In those days, to mark section corners, surveyors designated mature tree specimens as "witness trees." Usually their notes included comments on the nature of the land cover. GLO surveyors noted the presence of forest-covered ("timbered") areas, as well as prairies. In addition, they recorded the presence of barrens, scattering timber, and thin timber as transitions between forests and prairies. The thinly forested barrens were almost entirely maintained by frequent prairie fires that spread into adjacent woodlands. Only a limited number of tree species can survive that kind of stress, and they are fairly widely spaced.

According to Kilburn et al. (2009), the area occupied by the park, and most of the western half of Jersey County, were all within timbered vegetation at the time of settlement. Beyond the park in the eastern half of Jersey County, there was a more gently rolling topography, a mosaic of timber, prairie, barrens, and other transitional forms. After European settlement, the forests served as a source of lumber and fuel.

Plant Communities

The five categories below are based on a combination of substrate (soils), elevation, and exposure. The few dominant plants, indicated by an asterisk (*), can be considered as indicators, plants that are restricted to a community type.

Hill Prairies

On southwest-facing slopes of the park, on ridges that face the Illinois River, are loess-type hill prairies. They have variously been called bluff prairies, goat prairies, and prairie openings (Robertson et al., 1995). Growing mostly on Hamburg silt, these loess hill prairies are discontinuous grassland islands. They are restricted to a few places in North America, especially in Illinois along the Mississippi and Illinois Rivers. It is believed that these communities developed during the Hypsithermal period about 8300 years ago. During these warmer times prairies became dominant in Illinois. They occur on west-facing slopes that might otherwise be forested, but, due to exposure, wind, and well-drained loess-based soil, the habitat attracts more drought-tolerant plant types.

These communities are dominated by deep-rooted grasses such as little bluestem (*Schizachyrium scoparium**), Indian grass (*Sorghastrum nutans**), sideoats grama (*Bouteloua curtipendula**), lead plant (*Amorpha canescens*), purple prairie clover (*Petalostemon purpureum*), small-flowered scurf pea (*Psoralea tenuifolia*), heath aster (*Aster sericea*), showy goldenrod (*Solidago* *speciosa*), and purple prairie clover (*Dalea purpurea*). Prairie checklists for these small discontinuous tracts may include in the neighborhood of 40 species.

Dry-Mesic Upland Forest

Characterizing ridge tops as well as slopes that face south, southwest, and west, the predominant trees are 35–60 feet tall and 7–20 inches diameter at breast height (dbh). They include white oaks, black oaks,* yellow oaks, and mockernut hickories. Less common are post oaks. The understory includes smaller-stemmed members (8–20 feet tall and 1–6 inches dbh) of the above species as well as sassafras (*Sassafras albidum*), juneberry (*Amelanchier canadensis**), and flowering dogwood (*Cornus florida*). The sparse herbaceous layer includes scattered coralroot orchid (*Coralorhiza wisteriana*) and phlox (*Phlox maculata*).

Mesic Upland Forest

This community is found on middle portions of ravine slopes. Predominant trees are 45–80 feet tall and 10–25 inches dbh. They include red oaks (*Quercus rubra**) and white ashes (*Fraxinus americana**) plus scattered individuals of white oaks and red elms. Understory trees (15–20 feet tall and 4–9 inches dbh) are flowering dogwoods, conspicuous sugar maple saplings, and small-stemmed members of the dominant species. Among shrubs are colonies of wild hydrangeas (*Hydrangea arborescens*). The herb layer is better developed here and includes scattered Christmas ferns (*Polystichum achrostichoides*), false Solomon's seals (*Smilacina racemosa*), and coralroot orchid (*Coralorhiza wisteriana*).

Twin Peaks overlook—springtime view southeast toward the Illinois River valley. This is the park's largest tallgrass prairie and is maintained by periodic burning. Absent historically frequent fires, prairie ecosystems become forested on such slopes within a few decades.

Rattlesnake Trail. Rock outcrops line the trail near its eastern end.

Wet-Mesic Upland Forest

At lower elevations in ravines and along intermittent streams, the spicebush (*Lindera benzoin**) is usually common in the understory. Dominant trees (60–80 feet tall and 10–33 inches dbh) are sugar maples, red elms (*Ulmus rubra**), and sassafras. Common associates are basswood (*Tilia americana**), black walnut, and red oak. Closer to stream beds are sycamore, hackberry, and butternut. In addition to spicebush, the understory (10–20 feet tall) includes small-stemmed members of the above species plus pawpaw, ironwood (*Ostrya virginiana*), and wild hydrangea. The herbaceous layer is as rich as can be found in the region and includes Christmas fern, maidenhair fern, and interrupted fern (*Osmunda claytoniana*).

In this forest type, especially, you will find occasional giant trees, oaks ranging from 38 to 52 inches dbh, and of great height. Many have low branching patterns indicating an original open barrens environment when they were young trees.

Limestone Outcrops

These cliffs are of varying heights and occur along intermittent streams in many ravines. Ferns and herbs include walking fern (*Asplenium rhizophyllum**), bulbit fern (*Cystopteris bulbifera*), wild columbine (*Aquilegia canadensis*), shooting star (*Dodecatheon meadia*), cliff-brake fern (*Pellaea atropurpurea**), and wooly lip fern (*Cheilanthes feei*).

The walking fern, rare in this region, is found in valleys having rock outcrops. Many fern species survive well on weathered limestone faces.

ANIMAL LIFE

Because of varied habitats, ranging from riverside wetlands to dry ridge tops, the park and surrounding region are quite rich in species diversity. There are around 40 species of mammals, and over 200 species of bird life. Reptile and amphibian species, noted mostly from literature, and with limited direct observation, suggest the presence of 29 snakes and skinks, five salamanders, two toads, nine frogs, two turtles, and five lizards. (See plant and animal checklists beginning in Chapter 8.)

HILL PRAIRIES AND THEIR MANAGEMENT

This park showcases some outstanding examples of one of Illinois' rarest community types, the southwest-facing loess hill prairie. Significant for the survival of these remnants, our hill prairies are found on slopes varying from 17% to 56% grades, making the tracts historically too steep to plow or disturb productively. Where found, they remain as our last views of a vegetation type that once dominated the Illinois landscape.

Because the plants are adapted to dry (xeric) conditions on the slopes above the bluffs, the plant assemblages contain some species that are threatened and endangered in the state. Local growing conditions are more exposed and xeric than found in the adjacent forest behind the crest.

Work by Evers (1955) and Robertson et al. (1995) documented the fate of prairie openings over time from the 1930s to the present. At the time of the park's founding (1932) numerous prairie openings existed all along the bluff edges of the Illinois River, including many within the park. Recent comparisons of early literature and photographic records show that most of these prairie openings along the Illinois River can no longer be found. Between 1937 and 1974, McClain (1983b) found that an average of 62% of the original prairies were replaced by forests.

Why Prairies?

A major question for ecologists in the early 20th century involved why prairies exist anyway, especially in the east, coexisting with forested tracts. Three factors appear to be involved. The first is water balance. Forests do best in more humid regions, where precipitation exceeds evaporation. Grasslands do best where the opposite occurs, where evaporation dominates. Here we are more or less in balance, which is referred to by ecologists as an "evapo-transpiration ratio" of 1. Therefore, slight differences in solar exposure or protection will shift the balance toward prairie or forest.

Second, climatic history here is probably equally important. Well-developed grasslands, as tallgrass prairies, occurred as far east as Ohio several thousand years ago, an expansion that began during the Hypsithermal interval. The East became much warmer and drier then. Today, in Ohio and Indiana, remnants of that once continuous eastern grassland still remain as outliers or prairie remnants. This eastern grassland extension is referred to by ecologists as the prairie peninsula.

Camp Ouatoga's prairie in late summer. McAdams Peak is in the left distance.

Finally, there is evidence from past centuries that fire was quite frequent, caused by both lightning and American Indians. Humans used fire to drive game or perhaps to clear the vegetation from observation points. Because prairie species typically possess an extensive and deep underground root system, they can survive burning of the exposed parts. In fact, in areas where several fires occur per century there will be differential survival of those species that can tolerate this form of stress. Regularly burned areas at forest-prairie boundaries become savannas or barrens that include widely spaced tree species that were also fire resistant. Savanna vegetation once extended from northern Illinois to north Texas and included over 6 million acres of the Midwest (Anderson et al., 2007).

Due to the advent of Euro-American agriculture in the early 19th century, plowed fields formed extensive firebreaks throughout the Midwestern landscape, causing large wildfires to become quite infrequent and more local (McClain, 1983b). Earlier, wildfires often covered many square miles per event. As a result of much less frequent burning, woody plant encroachment began at the margins and worked inward, replacing the herbaceous prairie species by shading them out. Invading rough-leaved dogwoods, as well as about 17 other species that attract berry-eating birds, provide perching positions and thereby alter the microclimate. From their perches, birds pass through the seeds from shrubs and trees, initiating an expanding shrub zone at the edge, as well as within a prairie.

Also possible is the idea that climate change itself—a return to more equable conditions—has been a major factor in reducing grassland cover. However, evidence from tree-ring analysis and weather data tend to refute this. It seems that fire suppression is the most likely candidate for the precarious position of small prairies. The "Smokey Bear" campaign that began in 1944 also contributed to the end of burning over wide areas. For the park itself, beginning with the policies of the Civilian Conservation Corps, a fire-free period extended for 40 years from 1932, when the park was established (McClain & Ebinger, 2012).

In the present moister climate, without management of the remaining prairies, many species will continue to disappear from this otherwise diverse and interesting flora. Today, prescribed burns are the most effective tool in removing the woody plants that invade and eventually replace the prairie species.

Fire as a Management Tool

In 1977 the Illinois Natural Areas Inventory determined that 5 acres of high-quality prairie remained at McAdams Peak plus 4 acres of woody-encroached or somewhat degraded prairie (White & Madany, 1978). The McAdams Peak prairie was covered with a dense thicket of rank growth that included bittersweet (*Celastrus scandens*), raccoon grape (*Ampelopsis cordata*), Virginia creeper (*Parthencissus quinquefolia*), and crowns of numerous shrubs.

In 1973, personnel from the then–Illinois Department of Conservation (now IDNR) began prairie burns in the park, thus saving remnants that were endangered by over 40 years of fire suppression policy. Since that time, prescribed burns have occurred at least 10 times on McAdams Peak or Twin Mounds prairies. There is evidence of increasingly healthy populations of the tall prairie grasses as well as of the many other flowering plant species that are part of this ecosystem.

When considering the ecology of a region, one should also remember that this science has a historical dimension. What occurs now on this landscape is directly related to the events of past centuries and millennia. We will extend these observations to deep time in the following chapter introducing the park's geology.

Indeed, these descriptions can seem quite complex compared to the natural history of the surrounding countryside. But they also make this park one of Illinois' genuine treasures, justifying all efforts to continue its protection in perpetuity.

CHAPTER 5

PARK GEOLOGY

"Thus speak the stones, when all other things are silent."

– Carl Linnaeus

Unlike many regions of Illinois, Pere Marquette State Park is centered in an area exposing a complex geological history. While the area has been the focus of various research projects, mysteries remain that await future attention.

THE BIG PICTURE

Like the physical earth itself, the study of geology is multidimensional. For any region, the first thing you notice is its topography or surface relief. Technically called geomorphology or physiography, the surface form is modified constantly, sometimes by a dome or uplift, but mostly by ongoing erosion. Over thousands of years softer materials are the first to wear away, leaving harder and more resistant rock to define the higher elevations. This park is in one of the few counties in all of Illinois where cliff faces and road cuts reveal bedrock. Over most of the state, the bedrock is hidden from our view by the deep, glacially moved soils that cover the harder surfaces.

In Pere Marquette, and locally along the Great River Road toward Alton, we can examine a section of the earth where bedrock is revealed beneath the coating surface soils. Bedrock is a product of deep time. On scales of millions of years, thousands of feet of sediments were moved from high ground, via streams and rivers, and deposited in swamps, lakes, and ocean basins. Accumulating sediments were hardened into layers, where the uppermost are the youngest. Softer layers eroded away entirely, while harder, resistant ones have stood to the present day.

Using various tools, geologists can determine the age of rocks and interpret their sometimes tortuous history. Among the valuable clues are sequences of the rock layers, their physical and chemical features, and the presence of specific fossils, called indicator fossils. King (1982) provides an introduction to fossil identification.

Another dimension is crustal movement. From earliest times there has been compression, separation, folding, and faulting (cracking), where portions of the earth's crust move upward, downward, or laterally. All these actions have combined to produce an interesting landscape.

Note: Unfortunately, some geological terminology is unavoidable jargon. To help with understanding various terms, a glossary is provided at the end of this chapter.

The Surface

Soils are complex here in the park (see Chapter 4). In most regions, soil genesis begins with breakdown of the underlying parent material, rock particles weathered from local bedrock. In time, these physical particles are mixed with decayed organic matter from once-living plants and animals. The resulting mix provides a distinctive and local soil chemistry that, together with climate, influences which vegetation can live in a region.

At Pere Marquette, and on the high ground above adjacent river valleys, the situation is different. Here, soils are formed from deep accumulations of fine, post-glacial, wind-blown particles that arrived fairly recently from the north. Such mineral material has nothing to do with local underlying bedrock.

LOCAL GEOMORPHOLOGY

This park's geomorphology, with its average of 300 feet of relief, is mostly determined by its pre-glacial topography, in contrast to the mostly flat land just to the east. Below the ridgetop's wind-blown soils, we find an old landscape where eons of erosion have left behind only the hardest rock. The ridge of Calhoun County, across the Illinois River, has a similar history. The northern part is mapped by cartographers as part of the Lincoln Hills section of the Ozark Plateaus Province.

Glaciation Effects

As discussed below, glaciation during the Pleistocene epoch had a huge effect on the appearance of most of modern Illinois. In contrast, this corner of Illinois (westernmost Jersey County and adjacent Calhoun County) is one of three widely separated parts of Illinois that were never directly covered by glacial ice. The other two are (1) south of the Shawnee Hills in far southern Illinois and (2) the northwestern corner of the state that holds the title of the driftless section.

A number of questions beg for answers: What is the relationship of this area to the Ozark uplift? Why do rivers flow eastward here? But first let's consider what's directly beneath the park.

A LOOK AT THE BEDROCK

Beginning at the bottom (oldest rocks), we'll take a look at the inventory of what's here and what's missing.

PRECAMBRIAN ERA
(570 MILLION–OVER 3 BILLION YEARS)

Earth Section

ERA	SUB-ERA (years ago)	PERIOD	AGE		
			Animal	Plant	
Cenozoic (Recent Life)	Quaternary 2.5M-10,000	Recent	Mammals	Hardwood Forests	
		Pleistocene (Glaciers)			
	Tertiary 65-2.5 Million	Pliocene* Miocene* Oligocene* Eocene*		Conifers	
Mesozoic (Middle Life)	248-65 Million	Cretaceous* Jurassic* Triassic*	Reptiles		
Paleozoic (Ancient Life)	290-248 Million	Permian*	Amphib.	Spore-Bearing Forests	
	323-290 Million	Pennsylvanian*			
	354-323 Million	Mississippian			
	417-354 Million	Devonian	Fish		
	443-417 Million	Silurian		Algae – Seaweeds	
	490-443 Million	Ordovician	Marine Invertebrates		
	543-490 Million	Cambrian*			

Precambrian Rocks
underlie this region, 570 million to
3 billion years old.

* These periods are absent in this region.

*Time chart in color and see
detailed listing on p. 56.*

Rocks of this age are not exposed in the park region. These, the world's oldest rocks, are also called basement rocks. They are crystalline, igneous, and metamorphic. Basement rocks underlie most large land areas and are nearly always covered by accumulated layers (strata) of younger rock.

Worldwide, Precambrian rock varies in depth from 3500 to 20,000 feet. These formations are the remnants of cratons, fragments of a supercontinent that eventually broke up, leading to the continental shapes of today. This history is quite complex and beyond this introduction. Over eons, the North American craton, also called Laurentia, has been subject to downwarping, leading to incursion of shallow seas. In turn, erosion from higher ground has led to sediment accumulations throughout the Midwest and Great Plains that we now identify as the Paleozoic strata discussed below.

In Illinois, Precambrian rocks are not encountered anywhere near the surface. The nearest exposure is in the central Missouri Ozarks. From the very few drill holes north and south of here we find crystalline rocks of granite or rhyolite at depths of over 3000 feet. Their radiometric dates range between 1.3 and 1.4 billion years (Nelson, 1995). As such rock goes, our local basement rock is not particularly old. Some Precambrian rocks exposed in northern Minnesota have been dated at 3.0–3.6 billion years old. Another large exposure is found in the central Adirondacks of New York State. Worldwide,

Precambrian rock represents the longest time span of Earth's history. All such rock has been subject to high pressure and heat. For the period from 1.4 billion to 600 million ago years we find no record of geological events in Illinois.

THE PALEOZOIC ERA (543–248 MILLION YEARS AGO)

In the Midwest, above the Precambrian, the local succession of sediments or strata is about 3400–4000 feet thick.* Bedrock strata here are entirely from the Paleozoic era and range from the Ordovician period (490 million years) to the Mississippian period (325 million years). Strata underlying Jersey County and exposed in various places in Pere Marquette belong to four periods: Ordovician, Silurian, Devonian, and Mississippian. Although not present in the park, Pennsylvanian rocks are exposed about 10 miles to the east. (Wherever expected strata are missing among dated rock layers, the gap is called a disconformity or unconformity. This can suggest a period of erosion before the next period of deposition.)

This part of Illinois country is the western rim of the Illinois Basin, a regional structure shaped somewhat like the bowl of a spoon. The oldest sediments are deep in the center of the state, about 140 miles east of here. The sediments are shallower near the margins where some of the oldest strata surface in or near the park, the western flank of the basin. From here, geologists would say that the beds dip (tilt) eastward.

The Paleozoic era is so named because its sedimentary deposits were originally thought to be the oldest deposits containing fossils. We now know that earlier fossils do occur in some Precambrian rocks in a few places in the world. Paleozoic rocks, layered over basement rocks, are deposited to an average depth of more than 6000 feet under much of central Illinois in the spoon-shaped Illinois Basin. Repeated advances of seas were responsible for the gradual accumulation of marine deposits over hundreds of millions of years.

Cambrian Period (543–490 Million Years Ago)

While we find no locally exposed Cambrian strata, the period's legacy has certainly been felt. In this, the Paleozoic's earliest period, we find a variety of fossils that can be used to determine the dates of successively younger rocks up to the present.

In the mid-continent region there is evidence of rift valleys during the Cambrian period that formed when an ancient supercontinent began to break up. Referred to as Laurentia or "the North American Craton," the outline of

---

*Although the local topography is not nearly that thick, the beds slope, so stratum (layer) exposure accumulates as you walk across the surface, either "up section" or "down section."

this land mass bore no resemblance to the current shape of North America. Even though the rifts never spread and associated faults in the bedrock were later buried by hundreds of millions of years of sediments, the weaknesses left our mid-continent region somewhat unstable. Sometimes called failed rifts, the biggest of these is the Reelfoot Rift, where the New Madrid Fault shifted between December 1811 and March 1812. More than 1800 earthquakes of all magnitudes were generated. Of these, at least three were powerful enough to be rated at 7–8 magnitude on the Richter scale. At least 50,000 square miles were significantly rattled by these quakes in the comparatively empty landscape of that time. The greatest tremor was noted, or "rang church bells," as far away as Denver, Savannah, and Boston. Some worry that this ghost of the past could revisit, which should give us pause because of today's hugely greater regional population density.

After the Cambrian period, the region was covered at various times by shallow seas and, at other times, emerged as uplands. The undersea times are recorded as accumulated marine sediment deposits that provide the subsequent record to present times. They are dated and identified by the presence of indicator fossils of animals with hard parts, like shellfish. Their distinctive shells are layered in the rock during a restricted time period. Episodes of emergence (times above sea level) may be recorded as gaps in the sedimentary record.

On the Goat Cliff Trail, after the initial climb and looking to the southwest, the wooded slope covers the Ordovician Maquoketa shale.

Ordovician Period (490–443 Million Years Ago)

These are our oldest exposed sedimentary rocks, and they are classified among the following four strata.

Middle Series

Kimmswick limestone is 700 feet thick, coarse-grained, massive, exceptionally pure limestone. It is the uppermost layer of a series of hard limestones overlain by the soft Maquoketa shale. Its purity makes it especially susceptible to solution by percolating ground water. Being highly fossiliferous throughout, its crystalliferous crinoid stems yield a coarse granular texture. Farther south in Illinois, in the middle section of the Galena group, this stratum is a "pay zone," meaning a major oil-producing formation. To see the small example of this rock exposed in the park, drive northward up Route 100, about 0.8 mile from the visitor center parking area. On the east side of the road are small carbonate rocks close to the road level. These eroded and crumbling rocks are of Kimmswick limestone.

Upper Series

Maquoketa shale, 100–150 feet thick, crops out over a much wider area than any older formation (see box on following page). This cropping appears almost continuously along bluffs and streams for 5–6 miles north of the Cap au Grès monocline (noted below). Its shales are formed of fine siliciclastic sediments that were eroded from distant highlands, raised during the Taconian orogeny east of Illinois (Nelson, 1995). This series is nearly impervious to percolating ground water, which causes seeps or springs to emerge from its top surface. Water percolates downward through the overlying permeable limestone and then moves laterally until it emerges somewhere as a spring.

Formations occurring within the park*

Quaternary (Cenozoic) – Q (ca. 10 ky)
    Alluvium Qal
    Fan Q(f)
    Terrace Q(t)
~~~~~~~~~~~(Unconformity)

Mississippian – M (354–323 Mya)
    St. Louis limestone – Msl
    Salem and Warsaw limestones – Msw
    Keokuk limestone – Mk
    Burlington/Sedalia limestone – Mbk
    Chouteau limestone – Mct
    Hannibal shale – Mh
    Glen Park argillaceous, sandy, oolitic, shale – Mgp
    Louisiana limestone – Ml
~~~~~~~~~~~ (Unconformity)

Devonian (417–354 Mya)/ – D
    Cedar Valley limestone – Dcv
~~~~~~~~~~~(Unconformity)

Silurian (443–417 Mya) – S
    Niagaran dolomite (a.k.a. Joliet) – Sn
~~~~~~~~~~~(Unconformity)
Kankakee dolomite – Sk
~~~~~~~~~~~(Unconformity)

Ordovician – O (490–443 Mya)
    Brassfield limestone – Ob
    Edgewood (a.k.a. Bowling Green) limestone – Oe
~~~~~~~~~~~(Unconformity)
    Maquoketa shale – Om
    Kimmswick limestone – Ok

*Codes following names are keys that label geological maps.
For example, ky = thousand years; M = Mississippian; Msw = Mississippian Salem and Warsaw; Mya = million years ago.

The heavier and more resistant limestones and dolomites that overlie the Maquoketa often break and creep downward. Leaning trees and large strewn blocks are common features of the upper contact of the Maquoketa. Fresh surfaces on lower exposures are buffy gray, and on upper exposures they are greenish gray. Variegated coloring occurs in the upper 25 feet. There are very few fossils, but some trilobites are found where this formation outcrops in Calhoun County. As one ascends the Goat Cliff Trail, the Maquoketa shale forms the vegetated, alluvium-covered slopes to the left (west).

Edgewood limestone. Edgewood limestone, 10–50 feet thick, overlies the Maquoketa shale. Outcrops extend northward of the Cap au Grès monocline (or flexure) to more than a mile north of the village of Nutwood. Few fossils are present.

Brassfield limestone. Brassfield limestone, 10–30 feet thick, overlies the Edgewood limestone. It is a very hard, fine gray, finely crystalline to dense limestone. The few fossils are hard to remove.

The Silurian Period (443–417 Million Years Ago)

Probably one formation locally.

Niagaran Dolomite

The Pere Marquette Lodge is probably constructed of this stratum, although not all authors subdivide Silurian age rocks locally. Certain bridges and retaining walls, quarried in the vicinity of Grafton, are also probably of this stone.

Rock for the lodge was cut from the Callahan Quarry in Jerseyville Hollow at Grafton. Most impressive is the 700-ton fireplace of the lodge's Great Room. Rocks of this source were prized in the region as being dense enough to be dressed as large blocks that can support large structures.

By the time the lodge was expanded in 1999, these quarries had been closed for 20 years. Therefore additions to the lodge had to be built of rock quarried elsewhere.

Of special interest in the Niagaran is the famous Grafton trilobite, *Gravicalymene celebra*, which can be seen in several locations in the lodge. It occurs in the upper beds of the now inaccessible quarry. Look especially in the hallway between the Great Room and restaurant. Fossil burrows and trails can be seen in the stone flooring in and out of the lodge. Some silicified brachiopods have been enhanced by weathering of outside stone. See exhibits in the visitor center for geology and some fossils. Some 20 species of trilobites are found in the neighborhood.

The Keller Quarry, originally called the Grafton Quarry, was the last to operate in the Grafton area. It opened in the late 19th century and ceased operation in 1975. Located along Route 100 east of Grafton is a visitor center operated by the Grafton Chamber of Commerce, which contains more information on the geology of this area.

The Devonian Period (417–354 Million Years Ago)

One formation is present.

Cedar Valley Limestone (70–120 Feet)

This limestone forms all of the rock of this age common in southwest Jersey County. Brown to gray-brown in color, the rock is highly fossiliferous. In the lower parts it is soft, becoming progressively harder above (Walters et al., 2004).

Carboniferous System, Mississippian Series (354–323 Million Years Ago)

Eight formations are exposed in the park.

Louisiana Limestone (2–6 Inches)

This stratum is easily recognized and is hard, brittle, and very dense. It could be described as "buffy gray," a brownish gray to white on weathering. Exposures appear as a wall of masonry. Fossils, in the lower part, are hard to extract.

The Glen Park Formation (5–25 Feet)

Overlying the Louisiana, it appears as a series of thin beds of argillaceous sandy limestone, oölite, and shale. The upper parts are fossiliferous.

Hannibal Shale (Thickness Variable in Park)

Outcrops begin at the Cap au Grès flexure and run northward for 12 miles along the bluffs. It is thickest northward and thinnest southward, and characterized as soft, unresistant crystalline rock between harder, more resistant limestone or limestone dolomite. It is gray and relatively impervious to water.

The Hannibal stratum is said to be the source of geodes west of here, and possibly in this park (Ragan, 1999). Geodes are spheroidal globes, up to grapefruit size, with a hard, nodular surface of silica. An interior cavity has crystals, usually of calcite.

Chouteau Limestone (3.5–50 Feet)

The Chouteau crops out on the entire western edge of Jersey County. It is gray, hard, dense, fine-grained, cherty, and sometimes sandy. The presence of abundant calcite crystals is its main feature, and calcite geodes are common in parts of the formation. Abundant fragments of crinoid stems are scattered throughout, with other fossils being less abundant.

Sedalia and Burlington Limestones (200 Feet Combined)

Both strata are very fossiliferous, cherty limestone beds overlying the Chouteau. They form extensive outcrops comprising parts of the bluffs and nearly all of the uplands of the Hardin quadrangle. The Burlington caps the uplands and is the bedrock underlying wide areas. It is a hard, light gray and brown, cherty, crinoidal limestone resembling marble. The Sedalia, beneath the Burlington, is also a bluff-former. It is a massive, dolomitic limestone containing crinoids.

Keokuk Limestone (Thickness Variable in Park)

More coarsely crystalline than Burlington limestone, the Keokuk is more highly crinoidal in its lower parts. It also contains brown to gray calcareous layered mudstones ranging from 1 inch to several feet thick. The middle and lower parts have chert nodules, which are slightly darker gray than those in the Burlington. The considerable fragments of crinoids are diagnostically different from those in the Burlington.

St. Louis Limestone (75–185 Feet)

This relatively hard stratum is the resistant rock that crops out on steep bluffs and hillsides in or near the nature preserve (in the northern section of the park). The St. Louis is nearly pure limestone characteristic of Karst topography that develops in the overlying loess in flat areas of Calhoun County. It is dense, pale buffy-gray with nodules of brown chert in parts of the formation. At several sites this nearly pure limestone has been quarried for making lime. Bryozoans are the most frequent among uncommon fossils. The St. Louis and St. Genevieve limestones comprise the massive bluffs looming over the bike trail parking lot on the River Road just west of Alton. The cliff surface there exhibits the painted replica of the Piasa Bird.

STRATA NOT FOUND IN THE PARK

Pennsylvanian System (323–290 Million Years Ago)

The boundary of these strata is about 10 miles to the east. In the center of the Illinois basin, Pennsylvanian sediments accumulated up to 3000 feet as the basin gradually subsided. The extensive swamps of that period were later buried and became Illinois' extensive coal beds.

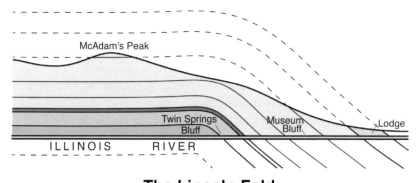

Sedimentary Rocks
350 Million Years Ago
(Before Folding)

The Lincoln Fold
The Same Rocks Today

(top) Strata diagram. (bottom) Strata at the Lincoln fold.

No sediments were formed.

Mesozoic Era (248–65 Million Years Ago)

No sediments were formed.

Cenozoic Era (65–1.8 Million Years Ago)

No strata are present of the type described to this point. We do have glacial loess deposits of the Pleistocene epoch in the park. This material, which directly overlies Mississippian limestones, is a windblown accumulation of fine particles. These are described in more detail later in this chapter.

During the Mesozoic and the earlier part of the Cenozoic eras, the surface of Illinois was exposed to prolonged weathering and erosion. The result, over a wide area, was a series of deep valleys causing much of Illinois to resemble the topography of this park, or the central Ozarks.

WHY DO THE ILLINOIS AND MISSISSIPPI RIVERS BEND SHARPLY EASTWARD AT THIS POINT?

Because of the collection of islands seen in the water at Grafton that captures our attention, it might be easy to overlook the fact that this area is the site of a major confluence: the place where the Mississippi River arrives and collects the flow of the Illinois River. The Mississippi rolls on with its volume increased by at least 22%.

Considering that the Mississippi and Illinois Rivers flow mostly north to south, their sharply eastward-angled course at this point has long been a source of conjecture. Just as odd, the Mississippi actually flows north just before meeting the Illinois River. This suggests the existence of significant structural deformities in the earth at this point, a story that needs to be told.

As seen on a regional geological map, we find that Pere Marquette State Park, located in the central Mississippi River valley, has its sedimentary strata dipping gently eastward, away from the central Ozark dome in southern Missouri. To understand why this is so, we should go back in time, looking toward the southwest, to see how regional events shaped southwestern Illinois' land surface.

The Ozark dome, or uplift, about 47,000 square miles in extent, is the highest, most dissected landscape between the Appalachian Mountains and the Rocky Mountains. Once part of a deep ocean basin, the land was uplifted in several stages by tectonic compression, beginning with the collision of the North American and South American tectonic plates in mid-Pennsylvanian times. Together these recurrent, asymmetrical uplifts are called the Ouachita orogeny.

Today's resulting dome surface is a highly dissected plateau where the high point, on its eastern side, is the St. Francois Mountains. At its core this area exposes Precambrian granites dating between 1.3 and 1.4 billion years. On most of the perimeter of the Ozark uplift are folds and normal faults. Some authorities hold that there has been no recent movement; others cite evidence for Late Tertiary and Early Quaternary activity.

FOLDS AND FAULTS

On the north end of the Ozark uplift are two major local structures believed to be significant in shaping the local landscape. These are the Lincoln fold and the associated Cap au Grès faulted flexure. The Lincoln fold, also called the Lincoln anticline in some sources, trends northwestward, parallel to the Mississippi Valley section between the park and Alton.

Cap au Grès Faulted Flexure*

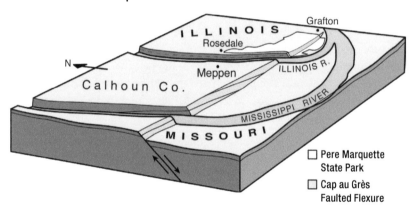

As the most prominent structural feature found in northeastern Missouri, the Lincoln fold follows its pronounced northwest to southeast trend for at least 165 miles. It is up to 13 miles wide. It divides the Illinois Basin on the east from the Forest City Basin to the west, and is believed to have developed in the Early to Mid-Paleozoic era. The Lincoln fold is an asymmetrical anticline, meaning that its northeastern limb has a barely noticeable gentle eastward slope. By contrast the southwestern limb dips steeply.

Superimposed on the Lincoln fold are faults and domes that make it complex to interpret. It shows structural (vertical) relief of up to 1000 feet. The Cap au Grès faulted flexure, which is aligned with the Lincoln anticline, arises on the southwestern flank of the anticline in Lincoln County, Missouri.

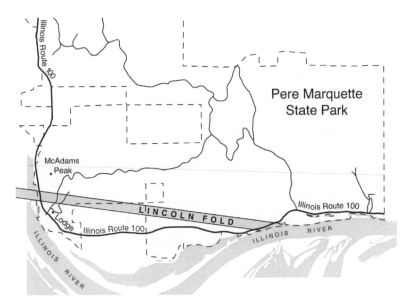

The Lincoln Fold*

It, too, extends about 165 miles to the west of this park. The fold and flexure swing eastward into Illinois and supposedly terminate in southernmost Jersey County, or possibly as far east as the SIUE campus. Locally, the steeply dipping bedding is overturned within the park, near the beginning of the Goat Cliff Trail.

The alignment of the Lincoln–Cap au Grès structure has suggested to many authors that much of the uplift along its entire length occurred during Late Mississippian to Early Pennsylvanian times. Structural relief is about 1200 feet in Illinois, and current thinking is that the movement has been entirely vertical. Steepest dips are up to 65° south, through vertical, to 65° north. Geologists, therefore, refer to it as an overturned structure. Because superficial features such as Pleistocene terraces have not been disturbed, no recent movement is thought to have taken place.

Digging Deeper

No doubt there is more to this story. A problem for this region is that there are too few drill cores that reach the Precambrian, as would be required to allow thorough analysis. Drilling to depths of 3000 feet is too expensive in the absence of a potential mineral payback. Therefore, there has not been a really comprehensive study of this structural phenomenon. The following

---

*This illustration and the three previous were drafted by R. W. Carter, park naturalist ca. 1948–1952.

is a summary of technical interpretations of several authors. This is not a complete review, but it is the best consensus so far.

It has been said that the Lincoln–Cap au Grès structure is a force fold over a high-angle reverse fault in the Precambrian crystalline basement. Another idea is that the Precambrian basement is cut by a continuous fault, along which the north side has been uplifted about 1000 feet, as suggested by data from magnetic and gravity surveys. Finally, some believe that there was an uplift of the northern block of the structure along a high-angle reverse fault in the Precambrian basement, plus force folding of the Paleozoic sedimentary cover. Tikrity (1968) has summarized that its genesis is similar to Laramide monoclines in the west, where sedimentary folds overlie faults in the Precambrian basement.

Nelson's (1995) review noted that the Lincoln–Cap au Grès structure has undergone recurrent movement. Initial uplift occurred in Devonian and Early Mississippian time, with major displacements continuing in Late Mississippian and Early Pennsylvanian time, as noted by angular unconformity along the flexure. Later movements tilted and displaced Pennsylvanian-age rocks. Nelson concluded that the tight relationship of the Lincoln anticline to the Cap au Grès faulted flexure "suggests that the anticline throughout its length is the surface expression of a fault in the Precambrian basement."

Approaching Consensus

Ancient faults, deeply buried though they may be, continue to be points of weakness in the face of later continental stresses. Wiggers (1997) noted that during Late Mississippian times the North American tectonic plate was colliding with Europe and Africa. This tectonic compression simultaneously caused the Alleghenies and Ouachita Mountains to be uplifted, as well as the Atlas Mountains in North Africa.

Whatever the full story, the Cap au Grès folded flexure, and the ancient movement of a deep fault, cause the waters to flow eastward as far as Wood River, Illinois, where once again they continue southward. Rivers follow the path of least resistance, and here we are left with a picturesque geological boundary. This is the best we can do to understand Pere Marquette State Park's L-shaped landscape.

WHAT ABOUT THE NEW MADRID FAULT?
WHAT EFFECT MIGHT IT HAVE HERE?

Occurring not so many miles south of the park, near the juncture of Tennessee, Kentucky, and Missouri, was the cluster of the New Madrid Earthquakes of 1811–1812. These quakes are notorious in the geological history of the Midwest, but were by no means the first such quakes in that seismic zone. Two of the three largest seismic shocks of the 1811–1812 winter and spring produced estimates of magnitude 7–8, and there were numerous smaller ones.

The New Madrid seismic zone is a complex of faults centered in the Reelfoot rift, where the crust of the North American plate began pulling apart about 500 million years ago (Ma). This is coincidental with the time when the Atlantic Ocean was being formed. A supercontinent, Rondinia (not at all resembling the present outline of North America), was breaking up, and masses of igneous rocks were intruded into the crust. Eventually the Reelfoot became a "failed rift," since no further crustal separation occurred there. In the intervening time, thousands of feet of sediments have buried this rift, leaving no surface trace—except for seismic instability.*

The question remains: What is the potential danger here of further seismic activity? Records of earthquakes in the last 20 years indicate that Pere Marquette State Park is just outside the northern edge of influence of the New Madrid seismic zone, which might indicate uncertain vulnerability. On the other hand, in 1895 a 6.8-magnitude earthquake centered in the New Madrid seismic zone, with effects extending from the Alabama border, up the Mississippi Valley to southeast Iowa, and east to southern Ohio.

We can't say for sure, but some geologists believe that seismic activity in the New Madrid zone is winding down. On the other hand, across Illinois, the Wabash Valley fault has produced at least three magnitude 5.0 or greater tremors in the last 20 years. In 2008, its 5.2-magnitude quake was felt as far away as Atlanta and Milwaukee (Hough et al., 2005). In that year, U.S. Geological Survey seismologists estimated a 7% to 10% chance of a 7.7-magnitude quake there within the next 50 years. Meanwhile, there has been almost no movement there for a lengthy period.

---

*Recent work suggests that the Wabash Valley fault that runs through White County, Illinois, 130 miles north of the New Madrid site, was also the source of major shaking.

FORMATION OF THE MODERN LANDSCAPE

The Quaternary Period (2.5 Million–10,000 BP)

The surface of the park and the soils that support the park's flora were formed by relatively recent events. Much of that time was occupied by the Pleistocene epoch, which lasted until about 10,000 BP. The times given below for the various glacial stages are approximate and vary among sources.

During the Pleistocene, this rugged border landscape just escaped being flattened and smoothed by the glaciations occurring between 2 million and 18,000 BP. There were various longer or shorter "interglacial stages" in which temperatures warmed enough to cause ice to recede from the landscape. The end of the Quaternary led to the Holocene, which is usually dated as beginning about 10,000 BP. Also, it marks the entry of humans into this region.

Thousands of years of weathering produced our modern soils, as the last glaciers receded and melted, and gradual re-vegetation occurred. Soil scientists can estimate closely the time since the last glacial presence by the depth of weathering, or oxidation, of the soil.

Continental Glaciation

Not for the first time in geological history, the earth began cooling about 2 million years ago. About 1.6 million BP the cooling led to increasing accumulations of ice over the Northern Hemisphere. Compared with today, the earth's mean annual temperature was cooler by 7°F to 13°F (4°C–7°C). This temperature drop is significantly large. Especially at high latitudes, it led to ongoing accumulations of ice and snow that failed to melt entirely during the cooler summers.

For centuries these accumulations continued to increase greatly in mass, becoming large ice sheets. They originated in Canadian centers east and west of Hudson Bay. Contrary to our daily experience with ice, given weight and time, glacial ice behaves as a plastic that can ooze over the landscape. The ice sheets grew and expanded southward many hundreds of miles from their original margins. Historically, glacial ages have lasted for 10 million or more years. On that basis we might conclude that we are only about one fifth of the way through the present glacial age.

The worldwide effect of precipitation accumulating as ice was huge. By some estimates, sea levels may have been lowered 300–400 feet below current levels. Ice sheet thickness in Illinois, typical of Pleistocene ice sheets at this latitude, varied locally between 200 and 800 feet. Temperature fluctuations allowed retreats (receding) of ice sheets after advances southward. Ice fronts advanced or receded, depending on the balance between warm temperatures and the rate of new snow accumulation. Low maximum temperatures at the glacial margin are necessary for ice sheet expansion.

Beginning with the oldest, the traditionally recognized stages (advances) are called Nebraskan, Kansan, Illinoian, and Wisconsinan. Within these four main advances, there is additional evidence, based on buried soils and glacial deposits, of about 23 additional advances and retreats. During the Pleistocene, glacial advances alternated with interglacial periods.

Causes?

It seems most likely that advances and retreats are timed in a complex way with the 100,000-year Milankovich cycle. To oversimplify, this cycle has three components that are based on variations in the shape of the earth's orbit, the tilt of the earth's axis, and the precession of equinoxes.*

The effect is to vary the contrast between winter and summer temperatures. While total solar radiation striking the earth is the same, energy partitioning between the Northern and Southern Hemispheres, and between high and low latitudes, is significantly affected.

Locally

For this neighborhood, it is sufficient to recognize three nearby ice tongues or lobes: Pre-Illinoian, Illinoian, and Wisconsinan. Using the depth of weathering measure, geologists and soil scientists have noted that Wisconsinan deposits, as expected, have weathered to the shallowest depth. Each glacial advance was followed by an interglacial stage with a climate more like that of today. During interglacial periods, thousands of square miles of landscape were re-exposed and gradually re-vegetated.

A Few Glacial Terms

As giant earth-moving machines, glaciers tend to level uplands and fill valleys in their paths. The resulting mixed earth and rock deposits are called glacial drift. Ice-laid sediments are called glacial till. A drift deposit may be called a moraine. Soil deposits formed beneath the glacier can be called ground moraines or till plains. Terminal moraines form at glacial boundaries and function frequently as earthen dams, impounding lakes during the melting phases. Earth berms formed along the sides of glaciers are called lateral moraines. When glacial materials are deposited by water, they are called outwash or outwash plains.

---

*Precession is the westward shift of autumnal and vernal equinoxes due to wobble or gyration of the earth's axis. This wobble has a period of 25,800 years.

THE LOCAL "PLEISTO-SCENE"

As noted earlier, Pere Marquette State Park and adjacent uplands of Jersey County were not covered by any of the major or lesser glacial stages. From the north and east there were advances into the eastern portion of Jersey County, but not into the park area or Calhoun County. Apparently the movement of ice sheets was stopped by deep trenches of the Illinois and Mississippi Rivers, and by the Lincoln anticline uplands. Even though there are no reports of ice sheets covering the park itself, the Pleistocene left plenty of other "tracks."

Pre-Illinoian glacial deposits (earlier than 310,000 BP) are deep and hard to find in Illinois, mostly due to obliteration by later stages. There are none known from the park area.

The Illinoian ice sheet (310,000–128,000 BP). Beginning about 270,000 BP, Illinoian ice advanced from the northeastern part of the state to the uplands of West Jersey County, passing beyond into the Illinois River valley but not encroaching the uplands of Calhoun County. East and south of here it extended about 130 miles, as far as Johnson County. Illinoian ice was probably about 700 feet thick, thinner than once believed but still impressive. Imagine an ice wall the height of a 65-story building and covering thousands of square miles.

In southwestern Illinois, Illinoian glacial drift, when present, is buried by the later arriving, wind-deposited, loess-based soils of Wisconsinan age. These accumulations are usually greater than 25 feet within the park. East of the park, in Jersey and neighboring counties, glacial drift of Wisconsinan age is usually less than 25 feet thick and does not entirely mask the underlying bedrock topography. This will be discussed in more detail later.

The Wisconsinan ice sheet also moved in from the northeast and reached its maximum advance about 24,000–23,000 BP. The ice only covered the northeast quarter of Illinois. By 11,500 BP it had retreated into Canada. The Wisconsinan was considered the coldest of the major stages.

During its retreat, the Illinois River was the main local meltwater drainage system. The river carried abundant rocks, sand, and finely ground "rock flour" that were deposited widely in the expanded floodplain of west central Illinois. The finer deposits were later windborne to become loess. During winters, receding waters left extensive exposed mud flats on the lowlands. Then, during dry periods, the finer soil particles were picked up by winds and deposited on the uplands.

Being the most recent stage, Wisconsinan glaciation left the most obvious effect on the Illinois landscape, especially on the landforms of the northern half of the state. The Woodfordian Substage, beginning about 22,000 BP and lasting about 5000 years, was the greatest advance of Wisconsinan ice. It was the major southeastern lobe of the Laurentide ice sheet that was centered in Canada, east of Hudson Bay.

LEGACY OF THE GLACIAL RETREAT

Around 17,000 BP the final retreat of Woodfordian ice began, forming huge meltwater lakes behind their terminal moraines. The lakes grew steadily in volume behind these earth and ice dams. The lakes were called Wauponsee, Watseka, Ottawa, and Pontiac. Behind their ice dams and moraines, these meltwater lakes inevitably, and often suddenly, collapsed beneath the weight of huge volumes of water. Think, for instance, of a suddenly collapsing dike, as seen on the news, during a major river flood. Such glacial meltwater floods, called torrents, carried great loads of sand and debris. Some sand deposits became the dunes in central Illinois. In some areas the deposits became sand prairies and bogs, a few of which remain upstate as part of the Illinois Nature Preserve system.

Approximately 90% of the soil materials of the Illinois landscape were deposited or modified by glaciers. Meltwater deposits, varying from gravels, sands, silts, or clays, tell geologists the story of runoff speed, and whether the water formed lakes or streams. In modern times these materials generally proved to be an economic boon for settlers who found glacier-modified soils to be generally fertile.

A Cataclysmic Event

About 1500 years into this glacial retreat (15,500 BP), accumulating meltwater in the largest lake finally overtopped and breached its moraine "impoundment." Thus began the short-lived but mighty Kankakee Torrent. Initially the water followed the Kankakee River channel, which led to the Illinois River valley. It has been called a flood of biblical proportions and was certainly a happening outside of historical human experience.

Add this scene to your catalog of natural disasters. Imagine you're sitting in a lawn chair atop McAdams Peak, in the middle of a wilderness, enjoying a lovely westward view across the Illinois River. Suddenly, within a 48-hour period, a wall of water the volume of Lake Erie comes crashing down the river valley, constrained locally by the park bluffs on the east and the spine of Calhoun County on the west.

During the Kankakee Torrent, the water rose approximately 180 feet above the Illinois River's present elevation. So great was the flood's force that huge chunks of Early Paleozoic bedrock were rolled down past the southern tip of the state. The flood blocked off the mouth of the Ohio River with 150 feet of boulder-laden debris that caused the Ohio to back up and eventually drain via its present channel to the south. Its ancient, original path is now the Cache River valley, as well as a cypress swamp just south of the Shawnee Hills.

A venerable guiding principle—covering much of geological interpretation—is that "the present is the key to the past." This is taken to mean that daily ongoing processes of uplift and erosion are responsible, in the long run, for most of the earth's physical appearance. But the Kankakee Torrent was one of a number of exceptions on the landscape, our local "Exhibit A," demonstrating what an exciting time the Pleistocene was.

A transition to the Holocene epoch followed the end of these glacial stages. In temperate and northern habitats worldwide, humans adapted to life in this newly exposed landscape. This theme is expanded on in Chapter 3, which discusses human prehistory.

Our Local Loess Deposits

In most places on earth, soils are formed gradually by the breakdown of subsurface parent rocks. Therefore, local soil chemistry will reflect closely the mineral characteristics of the local rock. However, about 70% of the soils in Illinois are formed of weathered wind-deposited soils. In Pere Marquette State Park particularly, the upland surface soils mostly have nothing to do with the local Paleozoic bedrock.

Also called aeolian (wind-deposited) soils, the particles were ground by glaciers from parent materials hundreds of miles to the north. The deposits are called loess (pronounced "luss"), from the original German word, and they are the principal substrates for many of our finest hill prairies and forested areas. Nearly everywhere they are regarded as agriculturally fertile, even if sometimes poorly drained.

Usually tens of feet thick here on the ridges, loess soils are composed mostly of light silt and clay particles in the average range of 20–50 micrometers (μm) in size. (There are about 25 millimeters, or about 25,000 μm, to the inch.) The deposits are deepest at the bluff edges all along the Mississippi and Illinois River valleys of the central and upper Midwest. They are composed of a variety of minerals including schist and feldspar, signatures of their origin from exposed Precambrian rocks hundreds of miles to the north. In older soils, particles of this size range tend to be "glued" together by calcium carbonate ($CaCO_3$). The lower (older) deposits are called Roxana silt and date from about 60,000–30,000 BP. The upper and most visible local deposits are called Peoria silt. They were formed during a short interval, probably between 23,000 and 12,500 BP.

A Puzzle

Why these specific ages, and why aren't loess deposits still forming? It turns out that a unique window of opportunity is required, a combination of factors allowing these deposits to form. First, as glaciers scraped and scoured the landscape, they ground and kneaded soil and rock into large quantities of rock flour or silt (2–64 µm diameter), along with soil materials of many other sizes. Secondly, the recently deglaciated lands south of the ice margin consisted of broad, sediment-filled river valleys. For a period these regions were sparsely vegetated and therefore largely unprotected from wind and water erosion.

Enter the Winds

Big ice sheets that remained north of the exposed area allowed the development of katabatic winds, dense, cold air flowing down a sloping surface of land or ice. The dense air is pulled down by gravity to lower elevations at speeds that can reach between 50 and 100 miles per hour. Today, such winds can be observed in a few places, such as running down the plateaus of the Greenland ice sheet. Antarctica provides another example. There, cold, dense air moves down ice sheets through the McMurdo dry valleys, heating upon descent, reaching speeds of 200 miles per hour, while evaporating all moisture in its path.

In the post-glacial Midwest there was a specific time window when glaciers had retreated northward. Just south of the glacial margin, the recently uncovered and unvegetated soil deposits dried out and were subject to high-energy katabatic winds. From the mix of exposed soil and rock particles, these north winds generated huge dust storms that carried the finest particles southeastward. As these dust storms rose over the bluff edges, a drop in pressure allowed the fine particles to drop out and accumulate especially deeply at the margins of the Illinois River valley. The deposits are usually deepest in such downwind landscapes of the east sides of Midwestern river valleys. Our own frame of reference would include the dust storms of the Great Plains, known in the 1930s as the "Dustbowl." However, the post-glacial dust storms would have been much more massive and longer lasting. At present the largely vegetated Midwestern landscape is much more windproof. It is better watered and, in the absence of great icy northern slopes, wind conditions are rarely violent.

A Note on Holocene Climate

About 10,500 years ago the general atmospheric circulation and sea levels were similar to those of today. But there have been many fairly abrupt changes in mean temperature and rainfall since the glaciers left. When the ice was in full retreat, the climate was still 5.4°F to 9°F (3°C–5°C) colder than today.

Between 7500 and 5500 BP, the temperature was 3.6°F to 5.4°F (2°C–3°C) warmer than today. It has been called the climate optimum or the Hypsithermal interval. The landscape was drier, which led to the widespread establishment of prairies in the Midwest, even as far east as central Ohio. After 5500 BP, a cooling period was established, including the Neoglacial, occurring between 900 and 400 BP. This overlapped with major European contact with North America. At the nearby Koster archeological site, there is evidence that it was drier in the intervals of 9700–5000 BP, 2100–1900 BP, and 1200–950 BP.

A SUMMARY AND SOME SPECIFIC LOCATIONS

Without considerable experience in field geology, most people would be hard-pressed to name the gray or somewhat tan bedrock and other strata that occur within the park. The following is a rough guide to what you are standing on, or facing, in specific places.

IN GENERAL

Within the park, most broad stream valleys are on Quaternary alluvium. As you proceed uphill toward a ridge, you cross undifferentiated Devonian/Silurian strata, then Mississippian limestone of the Chouteau formation. The ridge top is underlain by the Mississippian Burlington/Keokuk limestone. Keep in mind that the ridge-top soils are unusually deep in loess-derived soil. Only on the west-facing ramparts of the park that overlook the Illinois River valley can you find strata as old as Ordovician. They are exposed at the base of the cliffs.

THE GOAT CLIFF TRAIL

This trail has the best exposures of Pere Marquette's geological strata. From the northwest corner of the museum parking lot, proceed northward along the trail that parallels Highway 100. At the trail entrance, at highway level, you will see on your right the irregular cliff of gray and layered St. Louis limestone. The layers dip about 20° to the south. The lower part can be seen to be composed of angular fragments cemented into the surrounding limestone. This is called breccia. In one theory the strata were exposed to air in Late Mississippian times and then subjected to chemical expansion.

After following the road for about 100 yards, the trail angles away from the roadway and rises along a gentle gradient. Soon you come to a bench along a cliff face next to the trail. On the rock you find a U.S. Coast and Geodetic Survey benchmark. This spot is at the Cap au Grès faulted flexure on the right (east). Notice the steep dip (sloping angle) of the beds at this point. This first available outcrop exposes the Mississippian St. Louis limestone and the oölitic St. Genevieve (uppermost Mississippian, over the St. Louis limestone). The beds dip very steeply south here. On the left (west), a few paces beyond the benchmark, you come to:

Twin Springs

This is one of the few remaining trail-accessible springs that attracted original settlers to this area. It has been seriously altered, both by the building of the adjacent highway and of this trail. If only one trickle is visible, it is the northernmost.

At this site the much older Silurian marine carbonate rocks are exposed. This is the Niagaran dolomite. Devonian rocks are also exposed and cut by approximately five fault fractures close to perpendicular to the bedding. This is the Cap au Grès faulted flexure.

The water at Twin Springs probably flows from Ordovician-Silurian contact, which is obscured at this locality by the building of the trail. Groundwater, moving downward through porous Silurian rock, emerges here as a spring, since it is stopped from further downward percolation by the impermeable Ordovician Maquoketa shale.

Cap au Grès strata dip and benchmark.

Two formations are exposed at Twin Springs. The oldest, the Ordovician Bowling Green Dolomite (called the Edgewood Dolomite in some reports), is poorly exposed at the north end of the outcrop. The second is the Silurian Kankakee dolomite and the overlying basal Joliet, which form a prominent disconformity here and over a wide region.

Proceeding northward, up a slightly steeper grade, the beds become mostly horizontal and you gradually ascend through the Mississippian strata of Chouteau, then Burlington/Keokuk formations. The Ordovician Maquoketa formation is beneath the gentle, forested, west-facing slope on the left all the way to Goat Cliff.

Making an abrupt turn toward the east at Goat Cliff overlook and proceeding southward toward McAdams Peak, you cross Devonian/Silurian strata, then Mississippian Hannibal shale, then over Mississippian Burlington/Keokuk limestone to McAdams Peak. Although the Burlington/Keokuk formations cover most ridge tops as bedrock, directly underfoot near the cliff edge are fairly deep loess deposits, specifically the Peoria/Roxana silt. You climb through this exposure on an old 19th-century pioneer road cut on the approach to the crest of the ridge. At the top is the right turn leading to McAdams Peak's shelter and overlook.

From the Lodge by Car Northward and Uphill

The lodge foundation sits on Mississippian St. Louis limestone. The level ground around the lodge is the Brussels terrace, which is a former river level dating from Illinoian age. Proceeding upward, you cross: 1) Mississippian Salem and Warsaw formations; 2) Burlington/Keokuk limestone; 3) Chouteau limestone; and then 4) Burlington/Keokuk limestone, which continues along the ridge all the way to Tucker Knob. This same limestone underlies all other ridge tops. Notice a reversal in the stratigraphy: you drive "down section" on the way uphill. Thus, you start off at the top of the Mississippian, proceed downward, then ascend to Mid-Mississippian. This marks an anticline, beneath which is the buried thrust fault within Cambrian and Precambrian strata.

Other Locations of Interest

The marina area below the lodge is the Deer Plain terrace, an alluvium of Late Wisconsinan age. It is also exposed along the edge of the wildlife refuge running to the east.

At the campground, and proceeding eastward on Route 100 toward Grafton, the ground is a Quaternary fan for about 2 miles. Below this, along the river, is a Quaternary terrace.

Taking Route 100 northward from the lodge past the western edge of the park and parallel to the Illinois River, you drive close to the park's Paleozoic cliffs. Most of the cliff base is Ordovician Maquoketa formation, but beginning about a mile south of Rosedale, or 4 miles north of the visitor center parking area, the cliff base is of Devonian/Silurian age.

Where streams cross the highway from adjacent valleys, the roadway is built on Quaternary alluvium, or on Quaternary fans. If you turn right (east) at Rosedale, you drive over Quaternary alluvium. The road follows Coon Creek on the east edge of that alluvium in the lower reaches, eventually climbing at the edge of Lower Mississippian strata.

Camp Potawatomi, the group camp in Coon Valley, is underlain by Mississippian Chouteau/Hannibal strata. Walking downstream from the camp, which is Coon Valley, you move down section over exposed Devonian/Silurian strata, which are progressively covered by Quaternary alluvium.

Group camps Piasa and Ouatoga are on loess-covered ridge tops underlain by the Mississippian Burlington/Keokuk limestone.

Deerlick Hollow at the low end is Ordovician Kimmswick limestone. At higher elevations is the Ordovician Maquoketa formation.

Williams Hollow is underlain by Ordovician Maquoketa formation, but the highway crossing the mouth of the hollow runs on Quaternary alluvium.

Geologic Glossary

Alluvium: loose, unstratified sediments deposited by running water.

Anticline: an upward fold or arch of previously flat, stratified rock, formed by compression.

Argillaceous: rock containing a substantial clay component.

Basement rocks: the oldest rock formations, usually of the Precambrian era.

Bedrock: the hard, consolidated rock that underlies most soils of the planet.

Bryozoans: "moss animals"; tiny, colonial, aquatic filter-feeding organisms.

Calcite: carbonate rock, made of calcium carbonate ($CaCO_3$).

Chert: form of quartz rock, very fine-grained, high in silica.

Crinoids: invertebrate marine organisms, dating from 450 Ma to the present. Their variable flowery carbonate skeletons leave datable records in the strata.

Disconformity: a gap in the geological record where an expected stratum was either never deposited or was removed by erosion before the next deposition (synonym: **unconformity**).

Dolomite: similar in appearance to limestone; formed of calcium magnesium carbonate.

Dome: an uplifted area that dips (slopes away) in all directions (for example, Ozark dome).

Driftless section: an area in an otherwise glaciated landscape that was not covered by ice sheets.

Fault: a fracture or extensive break in the earth's strata. Faults often demarcate a tectonic plate boundary.

Faulted flexure: fault in strong strata, formed at low strain over preexisting faults or a weaker substratum.

Fold: a bend in originally flat strata due to pressure or compression.

Fossils, indicator fossils: skeletal remains of organisms that remain in rock strata. Many extinct species are indicators of a timeframe that allows identification of the stratum.

Geode: a more or less spherical, hard rock, usually of quartz, containing a hollow cavity lined with crystals.

Geomorphology: surface features of the earth, same as physiography.

Hypsithermal interval: post-glacial warm, dry period correlated with the final breakup of the Laurentide ice sheet. A new post-glacial atmospheric circulation was being established.

Indicator fossils: species whose skeletal remains in strata can be used to identify the various layers of strata.

Interglacial: periods between advances of accumulated ice on the landscape.

Intracratonic movement: formation of rift valleys; for example, the weakness at the Reelfoot rift that began in Precambrian times, 1.1 billion years ago.

Karst topography: a landscape formed over soluble rock strata where water can form sinkholes or caves.

Katabatic wind: a cold wind of dense air, pulled downslope by gravity.

Limestone: a rock material formed of calcium carbonate.

Loess: windblown, fine soil particles that often form deep deposits.

Monocline: a fold causing strata to dip strongly in one direction but remaining nearly level on the other side.

Oölite, oölitic: limestone formed of clusters of tiny spherical concretions, often called "egg stone."

Orogeny, orogenic belts: areas of former or current mountain building.

Parent material: the bedrock that breaks down to form the mineral component of adjacent soil.

Passive margins: the trailing edges of continents.

Physiography: surface form of the earth; geomorphology.

Platform: adjacent to shields but having sediments deposited usually by seaways; for example, our section of the Midwest and Great Plains.

Radiometric dating: many elements have naturally occurring radioactive isotopes. These decay at a known rate that can be measured, producing ratios that infer ages of strata.

Relief: measurable variation between ridge or hilltops and the adjacent valleys.

Rift zone, rift valley: a separation in the earth's crust due to tension in the continental plate.

Seismic zone: an unstable area of the earth's crust prone to earthquakes.

Shield: old, exposed Precambrian rock; for example, the Canadian shield, which extends to northern Minnesota, Wisconsin, Michigan, and the Adirondacks of New York State.

Siliciclastic (siliclastic): hard sediments, heavy in silica, formed after weathering of preexisting rocks.

Strata: beds deposited at the bottom of seas that eventually become layered.

Tectonic: forces that cause crustal movement or deformation.

Trilobite: extinct arthropods with jointed bodies, longitudinally three-lobed.

Unconformity: a gap in the geological record where an expected stratum was either never deposited or was removed by erosion before the next deposition (synonym: disconformity).

Weathering (soil): gradual breakdown and weathering of underlying rock. Soil is formed by the mixture of this mineral material with decaying organic matter.

CHAPTER 6

TRAILS

"Free-range chickens? Fine, but let's add free-range humans."

The trails in this guide have been measured by a wheel that records distances in feet. Doubtless you have no such device (and I can feel your relief already). But you are also given the total trail mileage, and you will remember that a mile is 5280 feet. So the measurements listed below will give you an approximate sense of your location on a given trail and the relative distance to the next feature. Mileage is also given for major features.

The park trail map (which follows the index) rates all of the trails as moderately difficult. The longer trails have level areas, but all trails have steep areas, sometimes including sets of steps. The shorter trails have a consistently steeper grade. As seen from the figures below, the elevation gain is 200 to 300 feet on virtually all of the trails. Below are figures, in feet, for some elevations within the park. Basically, what follows encompasses the variation.

Route 100 at park entrance	436
Lodge and Visitor Center	490–500
McAdams Peak	781
Twin Peaks	825
Dogwood Loop, highest point	625
Scenic Drive average	850

DOGWOOD TRAIL

Trail blaze:

Distance: 2944 feet (0.55 mile). This is a loop trail that begins to the right of and close to the old log cabin that was the former visitor center. This is a steep trail, but there are steps much of the way. The nature of this trail is that it climbs directly over the steep dip of the Cap au Grès faulted flexure. At this point, strata appearing nearly horizontal on the Goat Cliff Trail to the north are folded downward to a position many hundreds of feet beneath the surface. The best views over the river are in the winter, but it's a pleasant woodland walk anytime. Photos from the 1930s show that this route was largely prairie with occasional trees.

Feet

0–180   Fairly steep steps.

197   Trail fork to right. Choose either direction, but this description assumes counterclockwise and a right turn. From here a succession of steps over steeper areas alternates with a flat trail.

1000   Along the trail, on the left for about 50 feet is the most extensive and luxurious poison ivy patch I've seen anywhere.

1381   Northern (and highest) junction of this loop. Proceeding straight ahead is the Ridge Trail that arrives at McAdams Peak. Continuing on the Dogwood Trail, turn left and take the steps downhill, which proceed to a level section.

1774   Arrive at a shelter and guard rail that once overlooked a scene—and still does in winter.

2721   Arrive back at original trail fork.

2944   Arrive at starting point behind the cabin.

GOAT CLIFF TRAIL

Trail blaze:

Distance: 6739 feet (1.28 miles) to McAdams Peak overlook, then return trip via the Ridge Trail. Total round trip is 9213 feet, or just over 1.7 miles.

A summer view of the north end of the Goat Cliff Trail.

This trail is a good starting place for views of the Illinois River on the west end of the park. It also shows off the best views of the geological strata. Beginning at the northwest end of the visitor center parking lot, for several hundred feet the trail is level and follows the highway. Gradually it ascends the bluff and then parallels the highest cliff-forming rock walls found in this park. At its north end the trail doubles back, continuing a rise and fall, eventually rising to an overlook, down again, then to the McAdams Peak shelter overlook.

Feet

0   Parking lot trailhead. The first portion of the trail is relatively flat and parallels the highway.

832   Here the trail begins an upgrade and angles away from the highway. You will notice a surveyor's benchmark along the bordering rock face. The rocks cropping out at this point are part of the Cap au Grès faulted flexure. As you face the cliff, notice that the strata dip at a steep angle to the right.

A bench on the right is opposite a feature that was once very attractive to local pioneers: Twin Springs. Its beauty has been compromised by highway construction, but after wet weather, water can be seen emerging from two points. The water emerges above dense Ordovician strata and below the more porous Silurian rock. Continuing northward you walk up slope. Soil on the slope to your left (west) covers the Ordovician Maquoketa shale. When you see tree trunks here that slope in a downhill direction, it's a sign that general soil slumping has slowly undermined that tree's root system.

1562   The trail passes a large rock outcrop on the left that was once part of the cliff in the right-hand distance—another tribute to the force of gravity.

1760   On your right, through the woods, are Silurian cliffs, a yellowish cliff face, of dolomitic limestone. It is surmounted by the Hannibal shale slope, the lowermost Mississippian stratum.

3628   You are in the presence of the widest and highest cliff face in the park. The lower portions are Devonian strata: from the bottom are the Edgewood, Kankakee, and Joliet. Above those are the Mississippian strata, Hannibal shale beneath the Chouteau formation.

3727   You are passing a stump on the left next to the collapsed carcass of a large tree trunk. Until about 2001 it was one of the largest yellow oak trees in the state. As you can see, the hollow trunk weakened the tree mechanically, such that its fall was inevitable.

(*Side note:* It's interesting that many old trees in mature forests have heart rot. This is not necessarily a bad thing. Research has shown that hollow trees often produce roots that grow inward toward the base of a hollow. These interior roots will reabsorb the nutrients released from the heart rot process and recycle them into new growth, which gives these old specimens a competitive advantage. As we walk in the woods, our eyes show us how the upward growth of plants is a competition for the light, which makes photosynthesis—and survival—possible. But within the unseen world of the soil there is a keen competition with neighboring root systems for the sometimes scarce soil nutrients.)

3919   Rock face materials have partially blocked the trail. Be careful here, as the surrounding clay soil can be slippery.

An aerial view. To the right, Goat Cliff Trail follows the ridge in the right middle ground. To the left is Williams Hollow, mostly private property.

4243   (0.8 mile) You have reached the north end and last point where the trail continuously follows the west-facing woods. There are benches and a couple of overlooks where you can see across Williams Hollow, which includes private property. Across this valley a prairie opening can be seen to the north, and just beyond is the site of group camp Ouatoga.

At this point the trail doubles back to the south, and you will walk through a forest above an east-facing slope. Different tree species are more common on this moister, more protected area.

5399   Just over 1 mile. After following a flat area, the trail climbs again and forks. The right fork climbs to an overlook where you can see the slough named Lower Stump Lake of the Illinois River valley. The trail to the left bypasses this scenic overlook and continues to pass through woods.

From Blue Ash Overlook, an early spring view over Stump Lake and the Illinois River.

If you take the narrow right-hand trail, at the overlook you will see several small blue ash trees that typically have square twigs, hence their species name *Fraxinus quadrangulata*. They are frequently whacked back to protect the view. Being at the edge of its range, this species is rare and this site represents my only station for them in the entire region. The set of steps to the left leads up to a bench and high overlook. Behind the bench is an especially picturesque old pignut hickory tree. In front of you is a prairie remnant, which is maintained by periodic burning.

6197   Continuing south (down from the overlook) you come to a junction with the bypass trail. Continue southward over a level, ridge saddle area. After that the trail climbs through a cut in the loess material that forms about a 6-foot-high earthen cliff on both sides of the trail. This is probably the remnant of an old pioneer road, perhaps more than a century old. Characteristic of such fine-textured loess is its ability to form enduring straight cuts.

6739   (1.28 miles) You have reached a 5-trail junction. The short one to the west leads to the summit of McAdams Peak. The stone and wood shelter here was built by the Civilian Conservation Corps (CCC). The view overlooks Lower Stump Lake, a backwater of the Illinois River, which is just beyond. The ridgeline of adjacent Calhoun County bounds the western view. The peak itself is a piece of prairie remnant surmounting an Indian burial mound. Decades before the park existed, archeologist William D. McAdams removed many sets of human remains that were placed in collections of the Smithsonian Institution.

The other four trails are: 1) the Goat Cliff Trail that you just ascended; 2) the Hickory Trail to the east that leads to the top of Twin Mounds, which you can see from here and which proceeds to the junction of Hickory North Trail and Twin shelter. Then two trails lead downhill to the south, arriving near the visitor center: 3) the Ravine Trail moves downward and inland through a narrow valley and denser vegetation; and 4) the Ridge Trail is on higher ground that, in places, offers views over the river. Part way down it forks into an outer trail with river views, and an inner trail. Both are interesting.

RIDGE TRAIL

Trail blaze:

Distance: 2474 feet (0.47 mile) between the 4-trail junction at McAdams Peak and the visitor center parking lot. Treating the Ridge Trail as part of Goat Cliff Trail loop, it will be described from the top. As its name implies, the Ridge Trail runs along a spur of the main ridge, here and there providing views to the west. I will continue with the previous measurements.

6739   (1.28 miles) McAdams Peak junction of the four trails as listed in the sign.

7499   There is a trail marking sign.

7811   A junction and steps to the ridge.

8406   The summit of the Cap au Grès faulted flexure is on the right (west). Descend the bluff via a set of steep steps. Various old trees, including honey locust (sprouting huge branched thorns) and Osage orange, have been girdled with chain saws, probably to reestablish prairie vegetation on this site. Earliest photographs of this site show bluff prairie occurring here.

9213   (1.74 miles) Reach the visitor center parking lot, as measured from the Goat Cliff Trail round trip.

HICKORY SOUTH TRAIL AND HICKORY NORTH TRAIL

Trail blaze: Hickory south: ⬜ *Hickory north:* ⬛

Distance: 15253 feet (2.89 miles) on Hickory Trail south, then north, then Ravine Trail back to the visitor center. Described as a loop, elapsed time 2.5 hours.

On the south slope, this trail winds along the side of the main ridge, rising and falling through forested landscape, eventually achieving the top of the ridge and road. At the road the trail crosses and becomes the Hickory North Trail. Continuing through wooded landscape it winds down to a valley, then up the slope with its high point at a large Indian mound. Then it descends to the trail junction at McAdams Peak.

HICKORY SOUTH TRAIL

Feet

0   Beginning along the Scenic Drive road separating the visitor center and lodge, initially the trail is fairly level. There is a large hackberry tree exceeding 3 feet in diameter.

1201   A steep ascent begins. Ash and persimmon trees are nearby.

1375   Wooden steps were placed on what was an old pioneer road.

1631   Trail junction. Sign says that Hickory Trail S (continues) joined by the 150-foot-long Oak Trail that crosses the Scenic Drive to the north. Steps remain.

A Luna moth rests along the Hickory North Trail, a sight easily missed when your field of view doesn't include the ground.

1796   Passing the end of steps.

2273   In the past 500 feet the trail has leveled out, and there are a series of curves passing trees of various sizes.

2467   Climbing to a ridge via switchbacks through woods dominated by oaks, maples, and hickories.

2854   At the top of the switchback is an unmarked trail intersection. It has descended from a ridge above to the left, then proceeds down slope to the cabin area.

Hickory Trail, north side. A fall view of the canopy.

4527   In leafless seasons there are good views of the Illinois River and Calhoun County to the west. On the east side, a nearby overlook is adjacent to the road above.

5983   (1.13 miles) Trail junction: Hickory South Trail to the left joins the Fern Hollow Trail (marked by an orange star) that continues straight ahead and downhill.

6188   Hickory South Trail reaches the Scenic Drive. Cross the road, and just uphill to the left it becomes the Hickory North Trail.

Hickory North Trail

Feet

7066   Trail bends to the left. In the leafless season there is a view to the north of Williams Hollow, mostly a private tract. Large oaks live on lower slopes. About 200 feet in from the road, and down hill about 100 feet, is a possible champion white ash. It is very tall and has a diameter breast height (dbh) of 42 inches.

7622   The trail leaves the ridge via switchbacks, down slope, to enter a valley. Along the way will be an assortment of woody plants: basswood, sugar maple, sassafras, redbud, white ash, spicebush, and shagbark hickory. Christmas ferns commonly edge the trail.

8650   Trail reaches its lowest level and follows a creek for a short distance.

9073   After rain or snowmelt the trail becomes muddy and slippery.

10,809   (2.05 miles) After a gradual climb the trail emerges on the ridge. A great Indian mound, supported by a wooden wall, comes into view. One of the large oaks to the north has a dbh of 38 inches.

At this point you can take a short walk to the left and see the CCC-built Twin Shelter. Taking the right branch, the trail is described below.

Connection to McAdams Peak

Trail blaze: ♥

11,148   (2.11 miles) Trail junction. A large mound is on the left, and wooden barricades line both sides of trail. Sign says, "Road 1/10 mile." Hickory Trail to McAdams Peak to the right.

11,374   Small understory trees are a population of Ironwood (*Ostrya*) on a southwest-facing slope.

11,818   Approaching the prairie overlook. A trail to the right follows a lower elevation. Left fork approaches overlook with small Indian mound on the south side.

12,078   Top of Twin Mounds overlook. There is a small mound to the left and several acres of tall grass hill prairie below. This is the best prairie in the park and is perhaps the largest in the region. The Illinois River is seen in the distance. McAdams Peak shelter is seen to the right.

12,476   (2.36 miles) Trail junction of four trails.

12,637   McAdams Peak shelter.

RAVINE TRAIL

Trail blaze: ◆

12,793   (0.0) Entering the Ravine Trail from its summit. This is a continuous descent and steep in places. Continuing the Hickory loop distance, I include the start of the Ravine Trail as 0.0 at the 5-trail junction.

13,33   (540) Begin stone steps, originally installed by the CCC. Numerous small maples are poised to take over this forest.

13,583   (790) Ravine Trail junction with Ridge Trail. There are wooden railings and benches that need work.

13,944   (1151) For a short distance there is a wooden trail perched on the edge of the bank. The wooden retaining wall of 2 × 8 timbers on the uphill side needs work.

14,500 (2844) On the right (north side) is a small population of Carolina allspice or sweet shrub (*Calycanthus*), which has interesting maroon flowers in May. It is quite west of its southeastern U.S. native habitat.

15,253 (2460, 0.47 mile) Trail ends at visitor center.

Carolina allspice, Calycanthus. *These shrubs occur only at one site along the ravine trail. Mainly southeastern, this attractive plant may have been carried west by pioneers.*

FERN HOLLOW TRAIL

Trail blaze: ★

Distance: 7614 feet (1.44 miles). This loop trail extends to the east of the two Hickory trails. It connects to Hickory South Trail just below the Scenic Drive where the trail connects with Hickory North Trail. It crosses the Scenic Drive 1.5 miles, just beyond where it connects to the Rattlesnake Trail.

From the lodge, by car, you can park at the Flagpole overlook parking lot on the Scenic Drive, then walk downhill briefly to the entrance of the Hickory South Trail. Follow that for a short distance to the Fern Hollow Trail entrance. On the south side it extends down to lower elevations, then crosses the Scenic Drive. The north section resembles the Hickory North Trail, to which it finally connects.

Initially winding down into a valley, it curves back up to a low ridge just above adjacent farmland, then climbs through a maturing oak forest. It passes a nice view of the river valley, and the trail is more open than other, more wooded trails.

At the lower elevations you will see Christmas ferns on banks. Unfortunately, in places you will find a dense cover of Amur (bush) honeysuckle (*Lonicera maacki*), which has red berries in the fall. This aggressively spreading shrub, a native of Asia, was introduced into the United States in the last 100–150 years. It grows much more efficiently than many native shrubs, capturing their space in just a few years. Much of the understory of this park is being converted rapidly to this species, thereby reducing the native plant diversity. From the 1930s to 1996 the plant was sold and promoted commercially, and by the USDA Soil Conservation Service, for "habitat improvement." It's just one of many disastrous exotic introductions based on ecological ignorance.

Feet

0   Fern Hollow Trail entrance off the end of the Hickory South Trail, 210 feet from the road. The trail blaze is an orange star. You walk downhill continuously. Noteworthy are the many woody root systems exposed along the cut banks of these trails, a sign of the decades of erosion that have taken place.

780   The trail continues its downward slope. Uphill on the right at this point is a large white oak with low branches. Its branching pattern suggests it was open-grown in the early days when this was probably pasture land.

1219   Reaching a temporary level area with a number of cut-up ash trees.

2411   The low spot of the trail. It runs along low banks with nice growth of Christmas fern, named for the fact that it remains green in winter as well as the main growing season. This is a weedy woods emerging on former pasture land as belied by the numerous dead trees and box elders. The trail crosses a shallow drainage area, then curves and ascends steadily.

3101   A bench sits at the edge of the park that overlooks farmland. You can see Calhoun County's ridge on the horizon. More degraded woods surround the site.

5593   Top of the ascent. The trail descends gradually through mature second-growth oak woods with lots of horseshoe bends.

Fern Hollow South Trail. Notice the low branching pattern of this ancient white oak. It demonstrates that the tree grew to maturity in an open area.

5966   Mid upgrade. On the downhill side is a large white oak with low branches, with a 43-inch dbh, again signifying open growth in its youth.

6614   Crest of the ridge. Good second growth with some persimmon trees. Some ironwood, maples, and cherries. Note that persimmon and pawpaw trees often grow in groves, perhaps due to their heavier fruits not being dispersed as far.

7614   Junction of Rattlesnake Trail. Sign says that Fern Hollow reaches road in 1/10 mile.

RATTLESNAKE TRAIL

Trail blaze: ⊟

Distance: 2925 feet (0.55 mile). A one-way spur trail, extending from the Fern Hollow Trail, will be described here. It ends at the Scenic Drive. Duration: about 1 hour.

Feet

0.0   Beginning at its junction with the Fern Hollow Trail, this trail begins by descending gradually for a hundred feet. Then it bends sharply to the right and descends steeply down a short ridge through a mature second-growth forest.

1037   Trail reaches the low point, then proceeds relentlessly upward through a nice forest containing oaks and hickories.

1872   Trail reaches a major outcrop cliff on the left (uphill side). Just downhill from the cliff at this point is an unusual small tree, about 10-inch dbh with gnarly winged bark, typical of a very large and old sugar maple (*Acer saccharum*). Surprisingly, it is that species. Nearby is a very large dead black oak at 43-inch dbh.

Note that this and other decaying wood on the forest floor is home to numerous tiny organisms that return nutrients to the soil. The original oak-hickory forest of this park is being replaced slowly in most places by shade-tolerating sugar maples. It takes 20%–40% canopy opening for oaks to regenerate, a condition not present in most of this park. The trail proceeds gradually upslope following a line of limestone outcrops.

2824   The pitted rock outcrop grows aspleniums, a fern species that lives on rock cavities.

Not visited often, Rattlesnake Trail is very scenic.

3962   Rattlesnake Trail meets the Scenic Drive. The sign says the lodge is 2.25 miles to the west. A vertical post at the road edge identifies this trail. It is just east of the Lover's Leap parking area, surrounded by a mowed area.

Walking the road west to the point where Fern Hollow crosses the road is 2193 feet, about 0.4 mile.

4665   Point on road opposite center of overlook.

6155   (or 2.6 miles from beginning of the Fern Hollow–South Trail). Point where Fern Hollow Trail crosses the Scenic Drive.

FERN HOLLOW TRAIL, NORTH SIDE

Trail blaze: ⭐

Distance: 5158 feet (1.02 mile). This trail is much like the Hickory North Trail, moving up and down through mature second-growth oak forest. Beginning new distance measures.

Feet

0.0   On the uphill side of trail is a partially decayed log with bluish green–stained wood. The fungus, *Chlorociboria aeruginascens*, causes this stain, usually on the outer or sap wood. It usually infects wood that is already partially decayed. Classed as an ascomycete, the matching green fruiting bodies are rarely seen. The understory shrubs are spicebush.

1166   The trail ascends. A bench is found in mid-ascent.

1541   Point on trail opposite Williams Hollow, where a non-functional fence once bounded farm property. Mosses line the trail bank, and oaks of various sizes persist.

3750   Junction with Hickory North Trail. Turning left on the Hickory Trail brings you to the road and parking.

4669   Passing white oak, uphill that is ca. 40-inch dbh. This trail is a gentle grade and wide.

4877   Road is reached. Sign says, "Lodge 1 mile to the west." Uphill parking at the Flag Pole overlook. Just beyond that (east) is the Eagle Roost overlook.

5158   (0.98 mile) Reached Flag Pole parking lot.

Fern Hollow–Rattlesnake trails by this circuit have a total mileage of 3.8 miles. To return to the lodge by road from the Rattlesnake Trail junction would be 1.1 mile.

TRAIL HAZARDS

Especially when planning longer hikes, a small first aid kit should be on your packing list. Adhesive bandages will suffice for cuts and scratches. An ankle support wrap is also worth carrying for the occasional sprained ankle. In addition, you should be alert for the following four hazards.

1. Venomous Snakes (See also Chapter 12)

In the pit viper category, the park has both timber rattlesnakes and copperheads. These snakes have a distinctive geometric banding pattern, although the overall shade becomes darker with age. Also, they also have triangular-shaped heads when compared to non-venomous snakes, whose heads are narrow. They might be encountered anywhere in the woods, although, over many years in this region, I personally have never seen one. In case of a snake bite, the current recommendation is to leave the vicinity of the snake and place the patient on the ground so that the patient's heart is above the level of the bite. To the extent possible, remaining calm slows the movement of venom in the body. Studies have shown that trying to extract the venom using suction devices not only does not work, but is likely to cause more tissue damage. Ideally call 911. The patient should be evacuated carefully to a hospital that has antivenin for the snake in question.

Non-venomous bites, such as from a black snake or garter snake, do not require urgent care, but the person bitten should be treated for infection as soon as feasible. All such bites are septic.

2. Ticks

Several kinds of ticks are found throughout this region, and they are known to transmit a growing list of illnesses. In the park, your body will mostly encounter them when hiking off trail. They can land on the skin from contact with surrounding vegetation. Hikers should inspect their bodies for ticks at the end of the day, and the ticks should be removed before they attach. In any season it is wise to hike in the woods with long slacks or jeans, and keep shirttails tucked in. Before starting on a trail, it is effective to treat cuffs and socks with a DEET-containing spray.

Patch of poison ivy. The trail sides are often lined with this plant. Notice the difference from fragrant sumac: the terminal leaflet is extended. Young leaves are shiny.

3. Poison Ivy

This plant is quite common, especially in borders between woods and open areas. Learn to recognize it. "Leaflets 3, let it be." In case of skin contact, the rash-causing resin will develop an inflammation in about 24 hours. It is comparable to a burn; over-the-counter topical anesthetics are available to reduce the itching. Some people are not susceptible, but keep in mind that one can become allergic at any time in life. It is also possible later to get the resin on your skin by touching clothing or other items that came in contact with the plant.

4. Stinging Nettle

These woodland herbs, 1 to 3 feet off the ground, often grow along trails, especially in lower areas in the park. The leaves are coarsely toothed and the stems and leaves are covered with fine "hypodermic" white hairs. Bare skin that comes into contact with the nettle will develop an immediate stinging sensation. For most people the pain subsides in an hour or two and does not require treatment, but topical anesthetics will work.

CHAPTER 7

DRIVES IN PARK AND VICINITY

The following roads are logged or described in this order: Scenic Drive from Lodge and Visitor Center, Upper Park Road, Mail Box Road, Army Road, Graham Hollow Road, Route 100. The immensity of this park can be appreciated by the fact that the adjacent highway, Route 100, runs for 10 miles from the east end to the park's northern terminus. Much of the surrounding landscape is quite scenic and worth the drive, so the log ends with park circumnavigation. We begin with drives within the park with mileage listed at various points of interest.

SCENIC DRIVE FROM LODGE AND VISITOR CENTER

0.0   Leave lodge intersection. [GPS: 38.97293 × 90.54327] As one proceeds uphill to the ridge, the winding road goes through forest and buff-colored vertical road cuts that appear to be made of clay. These are exposures of the loess material deposited by wind on the uplands of this park. There are drop-offs and no guardrails on this somewhat narrow road. Proceed carefully.

Mertensia *(bluebells) patches are common in spring along higher reaches of Scenic Drive.*

0.8	Eagle Rest overlook and parking.
1.0	Flagpole overlook. Steps lead to the overlook, which is of a former prairie.
1.2	Unlabeled overlook with panoramic view, also of a former prairie.
1.4	Unlabeled overlook. Prairie could be rebuilt. Loess bluff (deposit) can be seen on the other side of the road.
1.8	Fern Hollow Trail crosses the road.
1.9	Pullout bordered by woods.
2.1	Lover's Leap Scenic Overlook. Take a right turn on a loop road to find parking at the summit. The woods are nice, but there's no place to leap from! The mowed area below faces west.
2.2	Rattlesnake Trail access at road edge. For access, park at the Lover's Leap overlook.
2.4	Former Nike Base entrance on left (closed).
2.9	T-junction [GPS: 38.9622 × 90.50262] with Upper Park Road to the left and Army Road to the right.

Sassafras, a mature specimen along Scenic Drive. Its very angular branching makes this tree species identifiable at any stage.

On Scenic Drive, an apolitical traffic guide.

UPPER PARK ROAD

3.4   Mail Box Road, junction on right. Picnic areas here and onward at intervals. Also restroom on left.

3.7   More picnic tables.

4.1   Junction (left) to former Nike Base (closed).

4.3   Junction of Potawatomi Road on right, with parking lot, picnic area, and rest room.

4.4   Continuing straight ahead is the entrance gate of the road to group camps Ouatoga and Piasa. A right turn leads to the entrance to Camp Potawatomi Road. These three camps have a central dining hall and kitchen and spur roads to primitive cabins. Access to the camps is available to groups by reservation only. The camps were built by the Civilian Conservation Corps (CCC) and originally proposed to provide nature experiences for inner-city youth. The adjacent fenced area at this intersection originally enclosed barracks for the Nike Base staff and later served as a short-lived environmental training center before it was razed.

4.6   Returning south from Potawatomi junction.

5.4   Mailbox Road (left).

6.0   Junction of Army Road (left) and Scenic Road to lodge (right).

ARMY ROAD

Originally built by the CCC, the winding, descending road was improved by the army during the Nike Base period.

6.1   Continuing on Army Road (southwest direction), within a block is a left-side parking area (one to two cars) for access to the trail-less "Little Giant City" valley.

6.5   Parking (right) for access to trail.

6.7   Parking area (left).

6.9   Parking at base of "Little Giant City" valley.

7.1   Junction with Graham Hollow Road and hunter check station.

GRAHAM HOLLOW ROAD

Just beyond this junction, on the left (east) the hillside was the site of barracks for the CCC workers in the 1930s.

8.0   Equestrian (horse trailer) parking on right.

8.4   Highway 100 junction; turning left:

HIGHWAY 100, TURNING EAST (LEFT) TOWARD ALTON

9.1   Pere Marquette commemorative cross on left, intended to commemorate the site where Joliet and Marquette first landed on the Illinois River shore.

9.2   Ski Lift Road and juvenile home on left.

10.8   Downtown Grafton and junction of Route 3 with Route 100.

11.7   Grafton Visitor Center and museum on left, just to the east of town.

19.5   Piasa Creek boat launch area and small riverside park.

21.5   Clifton Terrace traffic light.

26.1   Alton, flour mill and traffic light.

HIGHWAY 100, GREAT RIVER ROAD, MILEAGES FROM ALTON HEADING WEST

Stop sign at flour mill and foot of State Street.

0.8   Vadalabene bike trail parking area.

4.5   Clifton Terrace stoplight.

6.5   Piasa Creek Harbor.

10.9   Entrance road to Elsah village.

12.4   Entrance road to Chautauqua village.

13.6   Grafton sign and Raging Rivers Park.

14.3   Grafton Visitor Center.

14.6   Grafton town begins.

15.0   Intersection of Route 100 and Route 3.

16.2   Grafton north end.

16.6   Illinois Department of Juvenile Justice entrance. These impressive buildings were originally the H. H. Ferguson stock farm of the 1920s.

16.8	Stone cross on outcrop by highway on right.
17.5	Graham Hollow Road on right.
18.3	Brussels Ferry entrance on left.
18.4	Small parking area on right.
18.6	Entrance to Gilbert Lake refuge parking area and trail terminus.
18.9	Pere Marquette riding stables on right.
19.4	Duncan Hill Youth Tent Camp on right.
20.6	Pere Marquette State Park campground entrance on right.
21.1	Park main entrance on right.

Leaving the park entrance and proceeding north:

21.3	Leave north visitor center parking lot.
22.1	Rock outcrops, Ordovician strata, near highway.
22.6	Williams Hollow on right; on left Dabbs Road public access. Geologically, this broad plain is an alluvial fan.
24.8	Stump Lake public access road on left.
26.3	Northern terminus of the park. Parking lot on right for Mississippi River State Fish and Wildlife Management Area building. Also the beginning (northern terminus) of the "Meeting of the Rivers" scenic road. Rosedale Road entrance to the north, 100 feet on right.

CIRCUMNAVIGATING THE PARK, CLOCKWISE DIRECTION

0.0   Begin at visitor center parking lot.

1.4   Williams Hollow Road (right) and Dabbs Road (left) on the alluvial fan.

2.9   Parking at edge of Nature Preserve.

3.6   Stump Lake access.

5.0   Fish and Wildlife parking.

5.1   Fieldon Road, turn right.

5.4   Coon Creek approaches road.

5.6   Rosedale Road, turn right. Rosedale church, small white building, metal roof, on left.

6.5   Pass Warford Road on right. Continue on as Rosedale Road follows Coon Creek.

7.8   Road winds up and out of valley.

8.3   Ridge top; Meadow Branch Road enters on left, which is the end of Rosedale Road. Forests change to farms.

11.0   Four-way intersection. On right, Mailbox Road leads into park. Straight ahead is Graham Hollow Road. Turn left on Powerline Road.

12.0   T-intersection: Liberty Road on left. Take Powerline Road, which continues on right.

12.7   Parking area on right and entrance to trail on east side of park.

14.4   Rolling Ridge Road enters on right, more like a subdivision than rural settlements.

15.7   Powerline Road ends at stop sign. Turn right on Otterville Road; 200 feet to T-intersection with highway, Route 3. If turning right, cross upland and descend to Grafton, 3 miles.

If turning left toward Godfrey:

18.2   Elsah Road enters on right. Turn right through village of Elsah.

21.8   Elsah Road enters the Great River Road.

32.8   Flour mill stop sign at Alton.

CHAPTER 8

VASCULAR PLANTS OF THE PARK

Alice DeJarnett* & Richard C. Keating

Common names are offered for each species, even though such names are often misleading or inadequate. There are several reasons for this. Often it is because most plant species are uncommon and therefore don't have common names. The USDA supplies a "common names" list because some users require them. Very common plants have names that emerged as part of local folklore, and so they may vary throughout an extensive range. The common names offered here may provide some help when cross-checking with other guides and floras. The Latin names, followed by authorities, are based on defined rules and descriptions and are therefore the best source for verifying an identification. Well-known older names are in square brackets.

Listed here are the names of about 461 species of vascular plants, including a few subspecies, varieties, and hybrids, belonging to 102 families. The sampling was not comprehensive given the sheer size of the park. Doubtless there are corrections and additions to be expected in the future. Progress to date shows the presence of a rich and diverse flora. The nine largest families in terms of species occurring here are Asteraceae (62), Poaceae (52), Fabaceae (26), Lamiaceae (19), Rosaceae (18), Cyperaceae (14), Ranunculaceae (13), Liliaceae (13), and Scrophulariaceae (12).

The list's organizational sequence is as follows:

Ferns and Fern Allies

Conifers

Flowering Plants–Monocots

Flowering Plants–Dicots

Within these listings, families are alphabetical, as are genera and species within each family.

---

*The original fieldwork and the taxonomic compilation were accomplished by Alice DeJarnett (1993) as a Master of Science thesis at Southern Illinois University–Edwardsville. For this version some editorial changes and nomenclatural revisions were done by her mentor, R. C. Keating.

FERNS AND FERN ALLIES

Adiantaceae, Maidenhair Fern Family

Adiantum pedatum L., Northern maidenhair fern. June–Sep. Rich, moist to wet wooded slopes or ravines.

Cheilanthes feei T. Moore, Slender lip fern. June–Sep. On limestone rocks or cliff face.

Pellaea atropurpurea (L.) Link, Purple cliff brake. On limestone rocks or cliff face.

Pellaea glabella Mett. ex Kuhn, Smooth cliff brake. June–Sep. On limestone outcrops in woods.

Aspleniaceae, Spleenwort Family

Asplenium platyneuron (L.) Britton, Sterns & Poggenb., Ebony spleenwort. May–Sep. Dry to moist woods.

Asplenium rhizophyllum L., Walking fern. May–Sep. Limestone outcrops in moist woods.

Dryopteridaceae, Wood-Fern Family

Athyrium filix-femina (L.) Roth subsp. *angustum* (Willd.) R. T. Clausen, Northern lady fern. June–Sep. Rich, wet woods.

Athyrium pycnocarpon (Spreng.) Tidestr., Narrow-leaved glade fern. Aug–Sep. Moist woods.

Athyrium thelypterioides (Michaux) Desv., Silvery spleenwort. July–Sep. Rich, wet woods.

Cystopteris bulbifera (L.) Bernh., Bulblet fern. June–Sep. Limestone outcrops in moist woods.

Cystopteris protrusa (Weath.) Blasdell, Lowland brittle fern. June–Sep. Moist woods.

Onoclea sensibilis L., Sensitive fern. June–Oct. Rich, moist to wet woods.

Polystichum acrostichoides (Michx.) Schott, Christmas fern. June–Oct. Woods.

Equisetaceae, Horsetail Family

Equisetum arvense L., Field horsetail. Apr–June. Streambanks.

OPHIOGLOSSACEAE, ADDER'S TONGUE FAMILY

Botrychium dissectum Spreng., Cut-leaf grape fern. Sep–Nov. Moist oak-hickory ravines.

Botrychium dissectum f. *obliquum* (Muhl.) Fernald, Grape fern. Sep–Nov. Moist oak-hickory ravines.

Botrychium virginianum (L.) Sw., Rattlesnake fern. June–July. Dry to moist woods.

OSMUNDACEAE, ROYAL FERN FAMILY

Osmunda claytoniana L., Interrupted fern. Apr–July. Rich, moist oak-hickory woods.

THELYPERIDACEAE, MARSH FERN FAMILY

Phegopteris hexagonoptera (Michx.) Fée, Broad beech fern. June–Sep. Rich, moist to wet wooded ravines or lower slopes. [*Thelypteris* Adans.]

CONIFERS

CUPRESSACEAE, CYPRESS FAMILY

Juniperus virginiana L., Red cedar. Hill prairies; open woods.

FLOWERING PLANTS—MONOCOTS

ALISMATACEAE, WATER PLANTAIN FAMILY

Sagittaria latifolia Willd., Common arrowleaf. June–Oct. Shallow water.

ARACEAE, ARUM FAMILY

Arisaema dracontium (L.) Schott, Green dragon. May–June. Rich, moist, wooded ravines.

Arisaema triphyllum (L.) Schott, Jack-in-the-pulpit. Apr–May. Rich, moist, wooded ravines.

Jack-in-the-pulpit—common along trails, this is the young fruiting structure.

Commelinaceae, Spiderwort Family

Commelina communis L., Asiatic dayflower. June–Oct. Native to Asia. Moist, disturbed areas.

Commelina diffusa Burm f., Climbing dayflower. July–Oct. Disturbed, moist woods.

Tradescantia ohiensis Raf., Bluejacket. Apr–Aug. Dry woods.

Tradescantia subaspera Ker Gawl., Zigzag spiderwort. May–Aug. Rich, moist, wooded ravines.

Cyperaceae, Sedge Family

Carex albicans Willd. ex Spreng. var. *albicans*, Whitetinge sedge. [*C. artitecta* Mack.]

Carex albursina E. Sheld., White bear sedge. Apr–June. Moist, wooded ravines.

Carex amphibola Steud., Eastern narrowleaf sedge. May–June. Wet, river bottom woods.

Carex blanda Dewey, Eastern woodland sedge. Apr–June. Moist, wooded ravines.

Carex cephalophora Muhl. ex Willd., Oval-leaf sedge. Apr–June. Woods.

Carex conjuncta Boott, Soft fox sedge. May–June. Sunny river bottoms.

Carex glaucodea Tuck. ex Olney, Blue sedge. May–July. Dry woods.

Carex grayi J. Carey, Gray's sedge. June–Oct. River bottom woods.

Carex hyalinolepis Steud., Shoreline sedge. May–July. Sunny river bottoms.

Carex leavenworthii Dewey, Leavenworth's sedge. Apr–June. River bottom woods.

Carex molesta Mack., Troublesome sedge. May–July. River bottom woods.

Carex rosea Schkuhr ex Willd., Rosy sedge. Apr–June. Rocky woods.

Cyperus esculentus L., Yellow nut grass. June–Oct. Disturbed areas; horse pasture.

Scirpus pendulus Muhl., Rufous bulrush. June–Aug. Wet area, edge of parking lot.

Dioscoreaceae, Yam Family

Dioscorea villosa L., Wild yam. June–July. Dry woods.

Juncaceae, Rush Family

Juncus tenuis Willd., Path rush. June–Oct. Along trails, moist or dry.

Iridaceae, Iris Family

Belamcanda chinensis (L.) DC., Blackberry lily. July–Aug. Native to Asia. Roadsides; dry woods.

Sisyrinchium angustifolium Mill., Blue-eyed grass. May–June. Rich, moist woods.

Liliaceae, Lily Family

Allium canadense L., Wild garlic. May–July. Openings in moist, wooded ravines.

Allium vineale L., Field garlic. May–Aug. Native to Europe. Disturbed, dry woods; horse pasture.

Asparagus officinalis L., Asparagus. May–June. Native to Europe. Horse pasture.

Camassia scilloides (Raf.) Cory, Wild hyacinth. Apr–June. Moist, wooded slopes.

Erythronium L. sp., Dogtooth violet; trout lily. Apr–May. Moist, wooded ravines.

Hemerocallis fulva (L.) L., Orange day lily. June–July. Native to Eurasia. Roadsides.

Hypoxis hirsuta (L.) Coville, Yellow star grass. Apr–June. Moist, rocky woods.

Lilium michiganense Farw., Turk's cap lily. May–July. Rich, wet, rocky, wooded ravines.

Maianthemum racemosum (L.) Link, False Solomon's seal. Apr–June. Moist woods. [*Smilacina* Desf.]

Ornithogalum umbellatum L., Star-of-Bethlehem. Apr–June. Native to Europe. Moist, disturbed areas.

Polygonatum biflorum (Walter) Elliott, Solomon's seal. Apr–June. Woods. [*P. commutatum* (Schult. f.) A. Dietr.]

Trillium recurvatum L. C. Beck, Purple wake robin. Mar–May. Rich, wooded ravines.

Uvularia grandiflora Sm., Yellow bellwort. Apr–May. Rich woods.

Trillium recurvatum *is common in moist woods in the spring.*

Orchidaceae, Orchid Family

Corallorhiza wisteriana Conrad, Wister's coralroot orchid. Mar–May. Moist, rich woods.

Spiranthes magnicamporum Sheviak, Great Plains ladies' tresses. Aug–Oct. Hill prairie edges.

Poaceae, Grass Family

Andropogon gerardi Vitman, Big bluestem. July–Sep. Hill prairies.

Bouteloua curtipendula (Michx.) Torr., Sideoats grama. July–Sep. Hill prairies.

Bromus commutatus Schrad., Meadow brome. May–Aug. Native to Europe. Horse pasture.

Bromus inermis Leyss., Smooth brome. May–July. Native to Europe. Sunny river bottoms.

Bromus pubescens Muhl. ex Willd., Hairy woodland brome. June–Aug. Wooded ravines. [*B. purgans* L.]

Bromus tectorum L., Cheat. Apr–July. Native to Europe. Sunny river bottoms.

Cenchrus longispinus (Hack.) Fernald, Sandbur. July–Sep. Dry, sandy roadsides.

Chasmanthium latifolium (Michx.) H. O. Yates, Wild oats. July–Oct. Sunny openings in moist areas. [*Uniola* L.]

Cinna arundinacea L., Wood reed. July–Sep. Dry woods.

Dactylis glomerata L., Orchard grass. May–July. Native to Europe. Disturbed, dry, rocky woods.

Dichanthelium acuminatum (Sw.) Gould & C. A. Clark var. *fasciculatum* (Torr.) Freckmann, Tapered rosette grass. May–Oct. Openings in moist, wooded ravines.

Dichanthelium boscii (Poir.) Gould & C. A. Clark, Panic grass. June–Oct. Moist woods.

Dichanthelium clandestinum (L.) Gould, Deertongue. June–Oct. Openings in wooded ravines; dry, ridge-top woods.

Dichanthelium oligosanthes (Schult.) Gould var. *scribnerianum* (Nash) Gould, Scribner's rosette grass. June–Oct. Dry woods openings; edge of hill prairie.

Dichanthelium villosissimum (Nash) Freckmann var. *praecocius* (Hitchc. & Chase) Freckmann, Panic grass. May–Sep. Horse pasture.

Digitaria ischaemum (Schreb.) Muhl., Smooth crab grass. July–Oct. Native to Europe. Horse pasture.

Echinochloa muricata (P. Beauv.) Fernald, Barnyard grass. Aug–Oct. Near shallow water.

Eleusine indica (L.) Gaertn., Goose grass. June–Oct. Native to Eurasia. Disturbed areas.

Elymus hystrix L., Bottlebrush grass. June–Aug. Dry woods.

Elymus hystrix var. *bigeloviana* (Fern.) Bowden, Bottlebrush grass. June–Aug. Dry, wooded horse trail.

Elymus villosus Muhl. ex Willd., Hairy wildrye. June–Sep. Dry woods.

Elymus virginicus L., Virginia wild rye. June–Sep. Dry to moist woods; hill prairie remnant.

Elymus virginicus var. *glabriflorus* (Vasey) Bush, Virginia wild rye. June–Sep. Dry woods.

Eragrostis spectabilus (Pursh) Steud., Purple love grass. June–Oct. Disturbed edge of hill prairie.

Festuca subverticillata (Pers.) E. B. Alexeev, Nodding fescue. May–July. Dry, rocky woods. [*F. obtusa* Biehler]

Glyceria striata (Lam.) Hitchc., Fowl meadow grass. May–Aug. Moist woods.

Hordeum pusillum Nutt., Little barley. May–July. Moist woods.

Koeleria pyramidata [*macrantha*] (Lam.) P. Beauv., June grass. June–Sep. Moist, wooded slope.

Leersia virginica Willd., White grass. July–Sep. Moist woods.

Muhlenbergia racemosa (Michx.) Britton, Sterns & Poggenb., Marsh muhly. Aug–Sep. Disturbed edge of hill prairie; roadsides.

Muhlenbergia schreberi J. F. Gmel., Nimble will. July–Oct. Horse pasture.

Muhlenbergia sobolifera (Muhl.) Trin., Rock muhly. July–Oct. Dry to moist woods.

Phleum pratense L., Timothy. June–Aug. Native to Europe. Dry, wooded horse trail.

Poa bulbosa L., Bulbous bluegrass. Late spring. Native to Europe. Disturbed edge of lawn.

Poa compressa L., Canada bluegrass. May–Aug. Native to Eurasia. Dry woods.

Poa pratensis L., Kentucky bluegrass. Apr–July. Native to Eurasia. Horse pasture.

Poa sylvestris A. Gray, Woodland bluegrass. May–July. Moist woods.

Schizachyrium scoparium (Michx.) Nash, Little bluestem. Aug–Oct. Hill prairies.

Setaria faberi R. A. W. Herrm., Nodding foxtail. July–Oct. Native to Asia. Disturbed areas.

Setaria parviflora (Poir.) Kerguélen, Perennial foxtail. July–Sep. Near shallow water.

Setaria pumila [*glauca*] (Poir.) Roem. & Schult., Yellow foxtail. June–Sep. Disturbed areas.

Setaria viridis (L.) P. Beauv., Bristly foxtail. June–Sep. Native to Eurasia. Disturbed areas; roadsides.

Sorghastrum nutans (L.) Nash, Indian grass. Aug–Oct. Hill prairies.

Sorghum halepense (L.) Pers., Johnson grass. June–Oct. Native to Eurasia. Roadsides.

Sphenopholis obtusata (Michx.) Scribn., Wedge grass. May–July. Dry woods.

Sphenopholis obtusata var. *major* (Torr.) Erdman, Wedge grass. May–July. Moist, wooded ravines.

Tridens flavus (L.) A. Hitchc., Purpletop. June–Sep. Openings in moist, wooded ravines; disturbed areas.

× *Elyhordeum montanense* (Scribn.) Bowden, Mountain barley. June–July. Disturbed edge of hill prairie.

Smilacaceae, Greenbrier Family

Smilax rotundifolia L., Catbrier. Apr–May. Dry woods; moist, disturbed areas.

Smilax tamnoides L., Bristly greenbrier. May–June. Dry woods. [*S. hispida* Muhl. ex Torr.]

FLOWERING PLANTS—DICOTS

ACANTHACEAE, ACANTHUS FAMILY

Ruellia humilis Nutt., Wild petunia. May–
Oct. Hill prairies.

Ruellia strepens L., Smooth Ruellia. May–
Oct. Moist woods.

*Ruellia, common on
high ground in May.*

ACERACEAE, MAPLE FAMILY

Acer negundo L., Box elder. Apr–May. Moist
woods; disturbed areas; roadsides.

Acer saccharum Marshall, Sugar maple. Apr–
May. Woods.

AMARANTHACEAE, PIGWEED FAMILY

Amaranthus albus L., Tumbleweed. July–Sep. Horse pasture.

Amaranthus hybridus L., Slender pigweed. Aug–Oct. Horse pasture.

ANACARDIACEAE, CASHEW FAMILY

Rhus aromatica Aiton, Fragrant sumac. Mar–May. Dry woods; hill prairies.

Rhus glabra L., Smooth sumac. June–July. Hill prairies; roadsides.

Rhus typhina L., Staghorn sumac. May–July. Old fields; open woods; edges.

Toxicodendron radicans (L.) Kuntze, Poison ivy. May–June. Woods; field edges.

*Pawpaw, an understory tree found
on higher ground. Blooms are visible
on some trees in late spring.*

ANNONACEAE, CUSTARD APPLE FAMILY

Asimina triloba (L.) Dunal, Pawpaw.
Apr–May. Moist to dry woods.

APIACEAE, CARROT FAMILY

Chaerophyllum procumbens (L.)
Crantz, Wild chervil. Apr–June.
Moist bottomland woods.

Cryptotaenia canadensis (L.) DC., Honewort. May–Aug. Moist, wooded ravines.

Daucus carota L., Wild carrot; Queen-Anne's lace. May–Oct. Native to Europe. Woods; disturbed areas; roadsides.

Daucus carota f. *epurpuratus* Farw., Queen-Anne's lace. May–Oct. Native to Europe. Woods; disturbed areas; roadsides.

Osmorhiza claytonii (Michx.) C. B. Clarke, Sweet cicely. Apr–June. Moist, wooded ravines.

Osmorhiza longistylis (Torr.) DC., Anise root. Apr–June. Moist, north-facing slope woods.

Sanicula odorata (Raf.) Pryer & Phillippe, Black snakeroot. May–June. Wet, wooded ravines. [*S. gregaria* E. P. Bicknell]

Sium suave Walter, Water parsley. July–Sep. Shallow water.

Zizia aurea (L.) Koch, Golden alexanders. Apr–June. Moist, rocky woods.

APOCYNACEAE, DOGBANE FAMILY

Amsonia tabernaemontana Walter, Blue star. Apr–June. Wet roadside.

Apocynum cannabinum L., Indian hemp; dogbane. May–Aug. Dry to moist open woods.

AQUIFOLIACEAE, HOLLY FAMILY

Ilex verticillata (L.) A. Gray, Winterberry. May–July. Dry, rocky woods.

ARALIACEAE, GINSENG FAMILY

Aralia racemosa L., American spikenard. June–Aug. Rich, moist woods.

Panax quinquefolius L., American ginseng. June–July. Rich, moist woods.

ARISTOLOCHIACEAE, BIRTHWORT FAMILY

Asarum canadense L. var. *reflexum* (E. P. Bicknell) B. L. Rob., Wild ginger. Apr–May. Rich, moist, rocky woods.

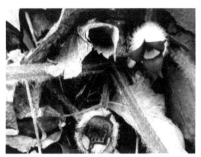 

Wild ginger flowers, close to the ground, are beetle pollinated.

Wild ginger—its heart-shaped leaves are unique in this flora.

ASCLEPIADACEAE, MILKWEED FAMILY

Asclepias purpurascens L., Purple milkweed. May–July. Open bluff top.

Asclepias quadrifolia Jacq., Whorled milkweed. May–July. Moist, rocky woods.

Asclepias syriaca L., Common milkweed. May–Aug. Horse pasture.

Asclepias verticillata L., Horsetail milkweed. May–Sep. Hill prairies.

ASTERACEAE, DAISY FAMILY

Achillea millefolium L., Yarrow. May–Aug. Native to Europe. Dry woods.

Achillea millifolium var. *lanulosa* (Nutt.) Piper ex Piper & Beattie, Western yarrow. June–Aug. Native to western United States. Hill prairie edge; horse pasture.

Ambrosia artemisiifolia L., Common ragweed. Aug–Oct. Dry woods openings; disturbed areas.

Ambrosia trifida L., Giant ragweed. July–Oct. Dry woods openings; disturbed areas.

Antennaria neglecta Greene, Pussytoes. Apr–May. Hill prairies.

Antennaria plantaginifolia (L.) Hook., Indian tobacco. May–June. Dry woods; roadsides.

Aster [see *Symphyotrichum* Nees]

Bidens bipinnata L., Spanish needles. Aug–Sep. Disturbed areas.

Brickellia eupatorioides (L.) Shinners, False boneset. Aug–Oct. Hill prairies.

Cacalia atriplicifolia L., Pale Indian plantain. July–Oct. Dry woods.

Cacalia muehlenbergii (Sch. Bip.) Fernald, Great Indian plantain. July–Sep. Moist, rocky woods.

Cichorium intybus L., Chickory. June–Oct. Native to Europe. Wooded ravine openings; roadsides.

Cirsium altissimum (L.) Spreng., Tall thistle. Aug–Sep. Dry, rocky woods.

Cirsium vulgare (Savi) Ten., Bull thistle. July–Aug. Dry woods; horse pasture.

Conyza canadensis (L.) Cronquist, Horseweed. May–Oct. Disturbed, moist woods.

Conyza ramosissima Cronquist, Dwarf fleabane. June–Sep. Dry roadsides.

Echinacea pallida (Nutt.) Nutt., Pale coneflower. July–Aug. Dry woods.

Echinacea purpurea (L.) Moench, Prairie coneflower. July–Aug. Moist, wooded ravine openings; horse pasture edge.

Eclipta prostrata (L.) L., False daisy. July–Oct. Shallow water.

Erigeron annuus (L.) Raf. ex DC., Daisy fleabane. June–Oct. Horse pasture.

Erigeron philadelphicus L., Fleabane. May–June. Moist, wooded ravines.

Prairie coneflower, a favorite among bee pollinators.

Erigeron pulchellus Michx., Robin's plantain. Apr–June. Dry to moist woods; roadsides.

Erigeron strigosus Muhl. ex Willd., Prairie fleabane. May–July. Dry to moist woods; disturbed hill prairie edges.

Eupatorium altissimum L., Tall boneset. Aug–Oct. Hill prairies.

White snakeroot, fall flower of the aster family.

Eupatorium coelestinum L., Mist-flower. July–Oct. Disturbed moist woods; disturbed former cabin site; horse pasture.

Eupatorium purpureum L., Purple Joe-pye weed. July–Aug. Dry woods.

Eupatorium rugosum Houtt., White snakeroot. July–Sep. Dry woods; horse pasture; distubed areas; roadsides.

Eupatorium serotinum Michx., Late boneset. Aug–Oct. Horse pasture.

Helianthus divaricatus L., Woodland sunflower. July–Sep. Dry woods openings; hill prairie border.

Helianthus hirsutus Raf., Bristly sunflower. Aug–Sep. Dry woods openings.

Helianthus strumosus L., Pale-leaved sunflower. July–Sep. Horse pasture edge.

[*Heliopsis helianthoides* (L.) Sweet, False sunflower. July–Aug. Dry woods; horse pasture.]

Krigia biflora (Walter) S. F. Blake, False dandelion. May–Sep. Dry woods; roadsides.

Lactuca canadensis L., Wild lettuce. June–Aug. Dry woods; disturbed areas.

Lactuca floridana (L.) Gaertn., Woodland lettuce. July–Sep. Woods.

Golden ragwort of the aster family. It often covers fields at low elevation in late spring. This patch appears just north of the visitor center parking lot.

Packera aurea (L.) Á. & D. Löve, Golden ragwort. April–June. Low woods and fields.

Parthenium integrifolium L., American feverfew. July–Sep. Dry to moist woods.

Polymnia canadensis L., Leafcup. June–Nov. Woods.

Ratibida pinnata (Vent.) Barnhart, Drooping coneflower. July–Aug. Hill prairies; horse pasture edge.

Rudbeckia hirta L., Black-eyed Susan. June–Sep. Dry to moist woods.

Rudbeckia triloba L., Brown-eyed Susan. Aug–Oct. Disturbed moist woods; roadsides; disturbed areas.

Senecio plattensis Nutt., Prairie ragwort. May–June. Dry woods; hill prairies.

Silphium laciniatum L., Compass plant; rosinweed. July–Aug. Hill prairie.

Silphium perfoliatum L., Cup rosinweed. July–Aug. Roadside ditch.

Solidago altissima L., Tall goldenrod. Aug–Oct. Roadsides.

Solidago drummondii Torr. & A. Gray, Drummond's goldenrod. Sep–Oct. Open bluff top below hill prairie.

Solidago flexicaulis L., Broadleaf goldenrod. Aug–Oct. Dry to moist woods.

Solidago nemoralis Dryander, Old-field goldenrod. Aug–Oct. Hill prairies.

Solidago rugosa Mill., Rough-leaved goldenrod. Aug–Oct. Hill prairies.

Solidago rugosa subsp. *aspera* (Aiton) Cronquist, Wrinkleleaf goldenrod. Aug–Nov. Fields; edges of woods.

Solidago ulmifolia Muhl. ex Willd., Elm-leaved goldenrod. Aug–Oct. Dry to moist woods; roadsides.

Symphyotrichum anomalum (Engelm.) G. L. Nesom, Blue-aster. Aug–Oct. Dry to moist woods; roadsides.

Symphyotrichum cordifolium (L.) G. L. Nesom, Blue wood aster. Sep–Oct. Wooded ravines.

Symphyotrichum drummondii (Lindl.) G. L. Nesom, Drummond aster. Aug–Oct. Moist wooded ravines; roadsides.

Symphyotrichum ericoides (L.) G. L. Nesom var. *prostratum* (Kuntze) G. L. Nesom, Wreath aster. Sep–Oct. Hill prairies.

Symphyotrichum lanceolatum (Willd.) G. L. Nesom, Tall white aster. Aug–Oct. Horse pasture.

Symphyotrichum lateriflorum (L.) A. Löve & D. Löve var. *lateriflorum*, White woodland aster. Aug–Oct. Dry woods.

Symphyotrichum oblongifolium (Nutt.) G. L. Nesom, Aromatic aster. Aug–Oct. Dry woods; roadside woods.

Symphyotrichum oolentangiense (Riddell) G. L. Nesom, Sky-blue aster. Aug–Oct. Dry woods; hill prairies.

Symphyotrichum parviceps (E. S. Burgess) G. L. Nesom, Small white aster. Aug–Oct. Hill prairies.

Symphyotrichum pilosum (Willd.) G. L. Nesom, Hairy aster. Aug–Oct. Hill prairies; horse pasture; roadsides.

Taraxacum officinale Weber, Common dandelion. Mar–Nov. Native to Europe. Disturbed, wooded ravines.

Tragopogon dubius Scop., Goat's beard. May–Jun. Native to Europe. Hill prairie remnant.

Verbesina alternifolia (L.) Britton, Yellow ironweed. Aug–Sep. Moist woods.

Vernonia baldwinii Torr., Ironweed. July–Sep. Hill prairie edges.

Vernonia gigantea (Walter) Trel. ex Branner & Coville, Ironweed. July–Sep. Horse pasture.

Balsaminaceae, Jewelweed Family

Impatiens capensis Meerb., Spotted touch-me-not. June–Sep. Moist, wooded ravines; roadsides.

Impatiens pallida Nutt., Pale touch-me-not. July–Sep. Disturbed areas.

Mayapple patches are common in woodlands. Its white blossoms are found in late spring. Blossoms and yellow fruits occur on stalks having twin leaflets.

Berberidaceae, Barberry Family

Caulophyllum thalictroides (L.) Michx., Blue cohosh. Apr–May. Rich, wet woods near seep (a minor spring).

Podophyllum peltatum L., Mayapple. Apr–June. Moist woods.

Bignoniaceae, Trumpet Creeper Family

Campsis radicans (L.) Seemann, Trumpet creeper. June–Aug. Roadsides.

Boraginaceae, Borage Family

Buglossoides arvensis (L.) I. M. Johnston, Corn gromwell. Apr–June. Native to Europe. Moist bottomland woods; open streambank.

Hackelia virginiana (L.) I. M. Johnston, Beggar's lice, stickseed. June–Sep. Opening in wet, wooded ravines.

Lithospermum canescens (Michx.) Lehm., Hoary puccoon. Apr–June. Hill prairies; dry "glade" in woods.

Lithospermum incisum Lehm., Yellow puccoon. Apr–June. Hill prairies.

Mertensia virginica (L.) Pers. ex Link, Virginia bluebells. Mar–June. Moist woods.

Myosotis macrosperma Engelm., Scorpion grass. Apr–May. Open bluff top.

Myosotis verna Nutt., Scorpion grass. Apr–May. Moist bottomland woods.

Brassicaceae, Mustard Family

Arabis canadensis L., Sicklepod. May–July. Disturbed areas.

Arabis hirsuta (L.) Scop. var. *pycnocarpa* (M. Hopkins) Rollins, Hairy rock cress. May–June. Disturbed areas.

Barbarea vulgaris W. T. Aiton var. *arcuata* (Opiz ex J. Presl & C. Presl) Fr., Yellow rocket. Apr–June. Native to Europe. Disturbed areas.

Capsella bursa-pastoris (L.) Medik., Shepherd's purse. Jan–Dec. Native to Europe. Disturbed areas.

Dentaria laciniata Muhl. (*Cardamine concatenata* (Michx.) O. Schwarz), Toothwort. Feb–May. Moist woods.

Descurainia pinnata (Walter) Britton subsp. *brachycarpa* (Richardson) Detling, Western tansymustard. Apr–June. Disturbed areas.

Rorippa sylvestris (L.) Besser, Creeping yellow cress. May–Sep. Native to Europe. Disturbed edge of lawn.

Thlaspi arvense L., Pennycress. Apr–June. Native to Eurasia. Horse pasture.

Cactaceae, Cactus Family

Opuntia humifusa (Raf.) Raf., Eastern prickly pear. May–July. Dry, open bluff top.

Caesalpiniaceae, Senna Family

Cassia marilandica L., Wild senna. July–Aug. Horse pasture; hill prairie borders.

Cercis canadensis L., Eastern redbud. Apr–May. Woods; edge of horse pasture; hill prairies.

Chamaecrista fasciculata (Michx.) Greene, Partridge pea. July–Sep. Horse pasture; roadsides; disturbed areas. [*Cassia* L.]

Red bud, of the pea family, is one of our earliest blooming spring trees.

Gleditsia triacanthos L., Honey locust. May–June. Disturbed bottomland woods.

Gymnocladus dioicus (L.) K. Koch, Kentucky coffee tree. May–June. Moist bottomland woods.

CALYCANTHACEAE, STRAWBERRY-SHRUB FAMILY

Calycanthus floridus L., Eastern sweetshrub. May–June. Native to southeastern United States. Moist, wooded ravines.

CAMPANULACEAE, BELLFLOWER FAMILY

Campanula americana L., Tall bellflower. June–Oct. Woods; roadsides.

Lobelia inflata L., Indian tobacco. June–Oct. Woods.

Lobelia siphilitica L., Blue cardinal flower. Aug–Oct. Moist woods.

Lobelia spicata Lam. var. *leptostachys* (A. DC.) Mack. & Bush, Spiked lobelia. June–Aug. Hill prairies.

Triodanis perfoliata (L.) Nieuwl., Venus looking glass. Apr–Aug. Moist, wooded ravines; open bluff top.

CANNABACEAE, HOPS FAMILY

Celtis laevigata Willd., Sugarberry. Apr–May. Roadsides.

Celtis laevigata var. *smallii* (Beadle) Sarg., Sugarberry. Apr–May. Bottomland woods.

Celtis occidentalis L., Northern hackberry. Apr–May. Wooded ravines.

Celtis occidentalis var. *canina* (Raf.) Sarg., Hackberry. Apr–May. Upland woods.

Humulus japonicus Siebold & Zucc., Japanese hops. July–Sep. Native to Asia. Roadsides.

Humulus lupulus L., Common hops. July–Aug. Roadsides.

CAPRIFOLIACEAE, HONEYSUCKLE FAMILY

Lonicera japonica Thunb., Japanese honeysuckle. May–June. Native of Asia. Edge of horse pasture.

Lonicera maackii (Rupr.) Maxim., Bush honeysuckle. May–June. Native of Asia. Disturbed ridge top and lower slope woods.

Sambucus canadensis L., Common elderberry. June–July. Roadsides.

Bush honeysuckle is a noxious invasive shrub that, each year, is taking over more understory in many wooded areas of the park.

Symphoricarpos orbiculatus Moench, Coral berry. July–Aug. Moist woods.

Viburnum rufidulum Raf., Southern black haw. Apr–May. Moist woods.

Caryophyllaceae, Pink Family

Cerastium fontanum Baumg., Mouse-ear chickweed. May–Sep. Native to Eurasia. Disturbed areas.

Dianthus armeria L., Deptford pink. May–Aug. Native to Europe. Horse pasture fencerow.

Silene latifolia Poir. subsp. *alba* (Mill) Greuter & Burdet, White campion. May–Sep. Native to Europe. Disturbed areas; field edges.

Silene stellata (L.) W. T. Aiton, Starry campion. June–Oct. Dry, rocky woods.

Celastraceae, Staff Tree Family

Celastrus scandens L., American bittersweet. May–June. Dry woods.

Euonymus atropurpureus Jacq., Burning bush. June–July. Moist woods.

Chenopodiaceae, Goosefoot Family

Chenopodium album L., Lamb's quarters. May–Oct. Disturbed areas.

Convolvulaceae, Morning Glory Family

Calystegia sepium (L.) R. Br. subsp. *americana* (Sims) Brummitt, Wild morning glory. June–Aug. Parking lot.

Convolvulus arvensis L., Field bindweed. May–Sep. Native to Europe. Horse pasture.

Ipomoea hederacea Jacq., Blue morning glory. June–Oct. Native to tropical America. Horse pasture.

Ipomoea pandurata (L.) G. Mey., Wild sweet potato vine. June–Oct. Horse pasture; roadside.

Flowering dogwood, a handsome understory tree common at higher elevations.

CORNACEAE, DOGWOOD FAMILY

Cornus drummondii C. A. Mey., Rough-leaved dogwood. May–June. Hill prairies; horse pasture.

Cornus florida L., Flowering dogwood. Apr–May. Woods; edges of horse pasture and hill prairies.

Cornus mas L., Cornelian cherry. Apr–May. Native to South Eurasia. Rocky lower slope woods.

CORYLACEAE, HAZELNUT FAMILY

Carpinus caroliniana Walter, Blue beech, musclewood. Apr–May. Moist woods.

Ostrya virginiana (Mill.) K. Koch, Eastern hop hornbeam. Apr–May. Moist woods.

CUCURBITACEAE, GOURD FAMILY

Sicyos angulatus L., Bur cucumber. July–Sep. Moist bottomland woods.

CUSCUTACEAE, DODDER FAMILY

Cuscuta campestris Yunck., Five-angled dodder. June–Oct. Roadside.

EBENACEAE, EBONY FAMILY

Diospyros virginiana L., Persimmon. May–June. Woods.

ELAEAGNACEAE, OLEASTER FAMILY

Eleagnus angustifolia L., Russian olive. May–June. Native to Eurasia. Disturbed slope woods; planted at extreme north end of park.

Ripe fruit of persimmon is found beneath trees in the fall. It's a favorite of raccoons.

Euphorbiaceae, Spurge Family

Acalypha virginica L., Three-seed mercury. July–Oct. Disturbed moist woods.

Chamaesyce maculata (L.) Small., Milk purslane. July–Sep. Disturbed areas; horse pasture.

Croton glandulosus L. var. *septentrionalis* Muell.-Arg., Sand croton. July–Oct. Horse pasture.

Euphorbia corollata L., Flowering spurge. May–Oct. Dry woods; hill prairies.

Euphorbia dentata Michx., Toothed spurge, June–Sep. Disturbed moist woods.

Fabaceae, Bean Family

Amorpha canescens Pursh, Lead plant. May–Aug. Hill prairies.

Amorpha fruticosa L. var. *angustifolia* Pursh, False indigio. May–June. Near shallow water.

Amphicarpaea bracteata (L.) Fernald, Hog peanut. Aug–Sep. Disturbed wooded ravines. [*Amphicarpa bracteata* var. *comosa* (L.) Fernald]

Astragalus canadensis L., Rattle weed. June–Aug. Hill prairies.

Baptisia alba (L.) R. Br. var. *macrophylla* (Larisey) Isely, Largeleaf wild indigo. May–July. Dry woods.

Dalea candida Willd., White prairie clover. June–July. Hill prairies.

Dalea purpurea Vent., Purple prairie clover. June–Aug. Hill prairies.

Desmodium cuspidatum (Muhl. ex Willd.) Loudon, Tick trefoil. July–Sep. Dry, rocky woods.

Desmodium glabellum (Michx.) DC., Tall tick clover. July–Sep. Roadsides.

Desmodium glutinosum (Muhl. ex Willd.) Alph. Wood, Sticky tick clover. June–Aug. Dry woods.

Desmodium nudiflorum (L.) DC., Nakedflower ticktrefoil. July–Aug. Dry open woods.

Desmodium paniculatum (L.) DC., Panicledleaf ticktrefoil. July–Sep. Moist woods.

Desmodium sessilifolium (Torr.) Torr. & A. Gray, Sessileleaf ticktrefoil. July–Aug. Prairies and open woods.

Lathyrus latifolius L., Everlasting pea. June–Sep. Native to Europe. Roadsides.

Lespedeza cuneata (Dum.-Cours.) G. Don, Sericea lespedeza. Sep–Oct. Escaped from planting; opening in dry woods.

Lespedeza violacea (L.) Pers., Prairie bush clover. July–Sep. Dry, rocky woods.

Medicago lupulina L., Black medick. May–July. Native to Europe. Dry woods.

Melilotus albus Medik., White sweet clover. May–Oct. Native to Eurasia. Openings in dry woods; disturbed areas.

Melilotus officinalis (L.) Lam., Yellow sweet clover. June–Sep. Native to Europe. Openings in dry woods.

Psoralidium tenuiflorum (Pursh) Rydb., Scurfy pea. June–Sep. Hill prairies.

Robinia pseudoacacia L., Black locust. May–June. Disturbed areas.

Securigera varia (L.) Lassen, Crown vetch. June–Aug. Native to Europe. Disturbed, former cabin area. [*Coronilla varia* L.]

Strophostyles helvola (L.) Elliott var. *missouriensis* (S. Watson) Britton, Wild bean. June–Oct. Shady roadsides; dry woods.

Trifolium campestre Schreb., Low hop clover. May–Sep. Native to Europe. Dry woods; horse pasture.

Trifolium pratense L., Red clover. May–Sep. Native to Europe. Roadsides; disturbed areas.

Trifolium repens L., White clover. May–Oct. Native to Europe. Disturbed areas.

Fagaceae, Oak Family

Quercus alba L., White oak. Apr–May. Upland woods.

Quercus ×deamii Trel. (probable hybrid of *Q. macrocarpa* and *Q. muhlenbergii*), Deam's oak. Apr–May. Upland woods.

Quercus macrocarpa Michx., Bur oak. Apr–May. Moist woods.

Quercus marilandica Muenchh., Black jack oak. Apr–May. Upland woods.

Quercus muhlenbergii Engelm., Yellow chestnut oak. Apr–May. Upland woods.

Quercus rubra L., Red oak. Apr–May. Upland woods.

Quercus stellata Wangenh., Post oak. Apr–May. Upland woods.

Quercus velutina Lam., Black oak. Apr–May. Upland woods.

Fumariaceae, Fumitory Family

Corydalis flavula (Raf.) DC., Pale corydalis. Apr–May. Moist woods.

Dicentra cucullaria (L.) Bernh., Dutchman's breeches. Apr–May. Moist woods.

GENTIANACEAE, GENTIAN FAMILY

Sabatia angularis (L.) Pursh, Marsh pink. June–Sep. Moist woods.

GERANIACEAE, GERANIUM FAMILY

Geranium carolinianum L., Carolina cranesbill. May–Aug. Open bluff top.

Geranium maculatum L., Wild geranium. Apr–June. Moist woods.

GROSSULARIACEAE, GOOSEBERRY FAMILY

Ribes missouriense Nutt., Missouri gooseberry. Apr–May. On rocks in moist woods.

HIPPOCASTANACEAE, HORSE CHESTNUT FAMILY

Aesculus glabra Willd., Ohio buckeye. Apr–May. Along creek in horse pasture.

HYDRANGEACEAE, HYDRANGEA FAMILY

Hydrangea arborescens L., Wild hydrangea. June–Aug. On rocks in moist woods.

HYDROPHYLLACEAE, WATERLEAF FAMILY

Ellisia nyctelea L., Aunt Lucy. Apr–June. Moist bottomland woods; disturbed areas.

Hydrophyllum appendiculatum Michx., Great waterleaf. Apr–July. Moist, rocky woods.

HYPERICACEAE, ST. JOHNSWORT FAMILY

Hypericum punctatum Lam., Spotted St. Johnswort. July–Aug. Dry woods.

JUGLANDACEAE, WALNUT FAMILY

Carya cordiformis (Wangenh.) K. Koch, Bitternut hickory. May–June. Moist to wet woods.

Carya glabra (Mill.) Sweet, Pignut hickory. Apr–May. Dry woods.

Carya ovalis (Wangenh.) Sarg., Red hickory. Apr–June. Upland woods.

Carya ovata (Mill.) K. Koch, Shagbark hickory. Apr–May. Upland woods.

Carya texana Buckley, Black hickory. Apr–May. Hill prairie border.

Carya tomentosa (Poir.) Nutt., Mockernut hickory. May–June. Dry to moist woods.

Juglans cinerea L., Butternut. Apr–May. Rich woods.

Juglans nigra L., Black walnut. Apr–May. Rich woods.

LAMIACEAE, MINT FAMILY

Agastache nepetoides (L.) Kuntze, Yellow giant hyssop. July–Sep. Moist, disturbed woods.

Blephilia ciliata (L.) Benth., Ohio horse mint. May–Aug. Along streams in horse pasture.

Blephilia hirsuta (Pursh) Benth., Wood mint. May–Sep. Disturbed areas.

Cunila origanoides (L.) Britton, Dittany. July–Nov. Dry, rocky woods.

Glecoma hederacea L., Gill-over-the-ground. Apr–July. Native to Europe. Along streams in disturbed areas.

Lamium amplexicaule L., Henbit. Feb–Nov. Native to Eurasia, Africa. Disturbed areas.

Lamium purpureum L., Dead nettle. Apr–Oct. Native to Eurasia. Disturbed bottomland woods; roadsides.

Monarda bradburiana L. C. Beck, Beebalm. Apr–June. Dry woods.

Monarda fistulosa L., Wild bergamot. May–Aug. Along streams in horse pasture.

Perilla frutescens (L.) Britton, Beefsteak plant. Aug–Oct. Native to Asia. Moist, rocky woods; roadsides.

Beebalm, a late spring woodland flower.

Physostegia virginiana (L.) Benth., Obedient plant. May–Sep. Dry woods; edges of hill prairies.

Prunella vulgaris L. var. *elongata* Benth., Self-heal. May–Sep. Native to Europe. Moist to dry woods; horse pasture; roadsides.

Pycnanthemum pilosum Nutt., Hairy mountain mint. July–Sep. Hill prairies; roadsides.

Pycnanthemum tenuifolium Schrad., Slender mountain mint. July–Sep. Dry woods.

Scutellaria incana Biehler, Hoary scullcap. June–Sep. Roadsides.

Scutellaria ovata Hill var. *versicolor* (Nutt.) Fernald, Heart-leaved skullcap. June–July. Rocky woods.

Scutellaria parvula Michx., Small skullcap. May–July. Hill prairies.

Stachys tenuifolia Willd., Thinleaf betony. June–Sep. Disturbed areas.

Teucrium canadense L. var. *canadense*, Germander. June–Sep. Moist woods; horse pasture; disturbed roadsides.

LAURACEAE, AVOCADO FAMILY

Lindera benzoin (L.) Blume, Spicebush. Mar–May. Moist, wooded ravines.

Sassafras albidum (Nutt.) Nees, Sassafras. Apr–May. Woods; borders of hill prairies.

LINACEAE, FLAX FAMILY

Linum sulcatum Riddell, Wild flax. May–Sep. Hill prairies.

LYTHRACEAE, TOOTHCUP FAMILY

Cuphea viscosissima Jacq., Blue waxweed. July–Oct. Horse pasture fencerow.

MAGNOLIACEAE, MAGNOLIA FAMILY

Liriodendron tulipifera L., Yellow poplar. Apr–May. Moist, wooded ravines.

MALVACEAE, MALLOW FAMILY

Abutilon theophrasti Medik., Velvet leaf. Aug–Oct. Native to India. Horse pasture.

Sida spinosa L., Prickly sida. June–Oct. Native to tropical America. Horse pasture.

MENISPERMACEAE, MOONSEED FAMILY

Menispermum canadense L., Moonseed. May–July. Moist woods.

MIMOSACEAE, MIMOSA FAMILY

Desmanthus illinoensis (Michx.) MacMill. ex B. L. Rob. & Fernald, Illinois bundleflower. June–Aug. Hill prairies; dry woods; roadsides.

MORACEAE, MULBERRY FAMILY

Maclura pomifera (Raf.) C. K. Schneid., Osage orange. May–June. Native to southwest-central United States. Upland and disturbed woods.

Morus rubra L., Red mulberry. Apr–May. Roadsides.

OLEACEAE, OLIVE FAMILY

Fraxinus americana L., White ash. Apr–May. Woods; hill prairies; horse pasture edge.

Fraxinus quadrangulata Michx., Blue ash. Mar–Apr. Hill prairie borders.

ONAGRACEAE, EVENING PRIMROSE FAMILY

Gaura parviflora Douglas, Velvety gaura. June–July. Native to western United States. Shallow water.

Oenothera biennis L., Evening primrose. June–Oct. Disturbed hill prairie areas; horse pasture.

Oenothera laciniata Hill, Cut-leaved evening primrose. May–July. Open bluff top.

OXALIDACEAE, WOOD SORREL FAMILY

Oxalis stricta L., Yellow wood sorrel. May–Oct. Woods; open bluff top.

Oxalis violacea L., Violet wood sorrel. Apr–June. Woods.

PAPAVERACEAE, POPPY FAMILY

Sanguinaria canadensis L., Bloodroot. Mar–May. Moist, rocky, wooded ravines.

PASSIFLORACEAE, PASSION-FLOWER FAMILY

Passiflora lutea L. var. *glabriflora* Fernald, Passion-flower. May–Sep. Wet bottomland woods.

Phytolaccaceae, Pokeweed Family

Phytolacca americana L., Pokeweed. July–Oct. Woodland openings; roadsides.

Plantaginaceae, Plantain Family

Plantago aristata Michx., Buckhorn. May–Nov. Horse pasture.

Plantago lanceolata L., English plantain. Apr–Oct. Native to Europe. Disturbed areas.

Plantago rugelii Decne., Broad-leaved plantain. May–Oct. Woods; disturbed areas.

Plantago virginica L., Dwarf plantain. Apr–June. Open bluff top.

Platanaceae, Plane Tree Family

Platanus occidentalis L., Sycamore. Apr–May. Wooded ravines; roadsides.

Phlox, or Wild sweet William, a common woodland flower in April.

Polemoniaceae, Phlox Family

Phlox divaricata L. subsp. *laphamii* (Alph. Wood) Wherry, Wild sweet William. Apr–June. Moist woods.

Phlox pilosa L., Downy phlox. May–Aug. Moist, rocky, wooded ravines.

Polygonaceae, Smartweed Family

Polygonum amphibium L., Water smartweed. June–Sep. Edges of shallow water.

Polygonum cespitosum Blume var. *longisetum* (Bruijn) Steward, Oriental lady's thumb. June–Oct. Native to Southeast Asia. Disturbed areas.

Polygonum hydropiperoides Michx., Mild water pepper. June–Oct. In or near shallow water.

Polygonum punctatum Elliott, Water smartweed. June–Oct. In or near shallow water; wet woods.

Polygonum scandens L., False buckwheat. Aug–Oct. Disturbed, moist woods.

Polygonum virginianum L., Virginia knotweed. July–Sep. Woods.

Rumex acetosella L., Sour dock. Apr–Aug. Native to Eurasia. Horse pasture.

Rumex crispus L., Curly dock. Apr–May. Native to Europe. Disturbed uplands.

Rumex obtusifolius L., Bitter dock. Apr–May. Native to Europe. Horse pasture.

PORTULACEAE, PURSLANE FAMILY

Claytonia virginica L., Spring beauty. Mar–May. Woods.

PRIMULACEAE, PRIMROSE FAMILY

Dodecatheon meadia L., Shooting star. Apr–June. Rocky, moist woods.

RANUNCULACEAE, BUTTERCUP FAMILY

Mature fruits of Baneberry or Doll's eyes. The entire plant is toxic. It can be found on the north side of the Fern Hollow Trail.

Actaea pachypoda Elliott, Doll's eyes. Apr–June. Rich, moist woods.

Anemone canadensis L., Meadow anemone. May–July. Rocky area near spring.

Anemone virginiana L., Tall anemone. June–Aug. Woods; edge of horse pasture.

Aquilegia canadensis L., Columbine. Apr–July. Rocky woods.

Clematis terniflora DC., Virgin's bower. July–Oct. Native to Japan and Korea. Disturbed former cabin area.

Delphinium tricorne Michx., Dwarf larkspur. Apr–May. Moist, wooded ravines.

Delphinium tricorne f. *albiflora* Millsp., Dwarf larkspur. Apr–May. Moist, wooded ravines.

Columbine.

Hydrastis canadensis L., Golden seal. Apr–May. Rich, moist woods.

Isopyrum biternatum (Raf.) Torr. & A. Gray, False rue anemone. Mar–May. Moist, wooded ravines.

Ranunculus abortivus L., Small-flowered crowfoot. Apr–June. Moist, wooded ravines.

Ranunculus hispidus Michx., Swamp buttercup. Apr–May. Woods.

Ranunculus micranthus Nutt., Rock buttercup. Mar–May. Horse pasture.

Thalictrum thalictroides (L.) Eames & B. Boivin, Rue anemone. Apr–May. Moist, wooded ravines.

RHAMNACEAE, BUCKTHORN FAMILY

Ceanothus americanus L., New Jersey tea. June–Aug. Dry woods.

ROSACEAE, ROSE FAMILY

Agrimonia pubescens Wallr., Downy agrimony. July–Sep. Woods; disturbed areas.

Agrimonia rostellata Wallr., Woodland agrimony. July–Sep. Woods.

Amelanchier arborea (F. Michx.) Fernald, Service berry. Mar–May. Upland woods; planted near visitor center.

Aruncus dioicus (Walter) Fernald, Goat's beard. May–June. Rich, rocky wooded ravines.

Fragaria virginiana Mill., Wild strawberry. Apr–July. Fields and open woods.

Geum canadense Jacq., White avens. June–Aug. Woods.

Malus ioensis (Alph. Wood) Britton, Prairie crab apple. May. Dry, rocky woods.

Potentilla recta L., Rough-fruited cinquefoil. May–July. Exposed bluff top.

Potentilla simplex Michx., Common cinquefoil. May–July. Moist woods.

Prunus mexicana S. Watson, Wild plum. Hill prairie edge; edge of ridge-top parking area.

Prunus munsoniana W. Wight & Hedrick, Wild goose plum. Mar–Apr. Moist bottomland woods.

Prunus serotina Ehrh., Black cherry. May. Upland woods.

Rosa arkansana Porter var. *suffulta* (Greene) Cockerell, Prairie rose. June–July. Hill prairies.

Rosa carolina L., Pasture rose. May–July. Dry woods.

Rosa multiflora Thunb. ex Murray, Multiflora rose. May–June. Native to China and Japan. Disturbed areas.

Rosa setigera Michx., Prairie rose. June–July. Dry woods.

Rubus allegheniensis Porter, Common blackberry. May–June. Woods.

Rubus occidentalis L., Black raspberry. May–June. Woods.

Rubiaceae, Madder Family

Cephalanthus occidentalis L., Buttonbush. June–Aug. Shallow water.

Galium aparine L., Catchweed bedstraw. May–July. Moist bottomland woods; disturbed areas.

Galium concinnum Torr. & A. Gray, Shining bedstraw. June–July. Dry to moist woods.

Galium triflorum Michx., Fragrant bedstraw. May–Sep. Moist woods.

Hedyotis nigricans (Lam.) Fosberg, Narrow-leaved bluets. May–Oct. Hill prairies.

Rutaceae, Citrus Family

Ptelea trifoliata L., Wafer ash. May–July. Hill prairies; edge of horse pasture.

Salicaceae, Willow Family

Populus deltoides W. Bartram ex Marshall, Eastern cottonwood. Mar–Apr. Roadsides; disturbed moist areas.

Salix exigua Nutt., Sandbar willow. Apr–May. Streambanks.

Salix nigra Marshall, Black willow. Apr–May. Shallow water; wet ground.

Saxifragaceae, Saxifrage Family

Heuchera americana L. var. *hirsuticaulis* (Wheelock) Rosend., Butters & Lakela, Tall alum root. May–June. On rocks in moist woods.

SCROPHULARIACEAE, FIGWORT FAMILY

Agalinis aspera (Douglas ex Benth.) Britton, Rough false foxglove. Aug–Sep. Hill prairies.

Aureolaria grandiflora (Benth.) Pennell var. *pulchra* Pennell, Yellow false foxglove. July–Sep. Hill prairies.

Dasistoma macrophylla (Nutt.) Raf., Mullein foxglove. June–Sep. Dry to moist woods.

Mimulus alatus Sol., Winged monkey flower. June–Sep. Streambank in moist woods.

Pedicularis canadensis L., Common lousewort. Apr–June. Moist, rocky woods.

Penstemon pallidus Small, Pale beard-tongue. Apr–July. Hill prairies; roadsides.

Scrophularia marilandica L., Figwort. July–Oct. Moist to wet open woods.

Verbascum thapsus L., Mullein. May–Sep. Native of Europe. Disturbed hill prairie remnant.

Veronica arvensis L., Corn speedwell. Mar–Aug. Native to Europe. Disturbed areas.

Veronica peregrina L., White speedwell. Apr–Aug. Horse pasture; disturbed areas.

Veronicastrum virginicum (L.) Farw., Culver's root. June–Sep. Dry woods.

SIMAROUBACEAE, QUASSIA FAMILY

Ailanthus altissima (Mill.) Swingle, Tree-of-heaven. June–July. Native to Asia. Roadsides.

SOLANACEAE, NIGHTSHADE FAMILY

Physalis virginiana Mill., Ground cherry. May–Aug. Horse pasture; roadsides.

Solanum carolinense L., Horse nettle. June–Oct. Disturbed areas.

Solanum ptycanthum Dunal, Black nightshade. May–Nov. Disturbed opening in moist woods.

STAPHYLEACEAE, BLADDERNUT FAMILY

Staphylea trifoliata Marshall, Bladdernut. Apr–May. Moist, rocky woods.

Tiliaceae, Linden Family

Tilia americana L., American basswood. May–July. Dry woods.

Ulmaceae, Elm Family

Ulmus rubra Muhl., Slippery elm. Feb–Apr. Woods.

Urticaceae, Nettle Family

Boehmeria cylindrica (L.) Sw., False nettle. July–Oct. Upland woods.

Laportea canadensis (L.) Wedd., Wood nettle. June–Sep. Moist, wooded ravines.

Pilea pumila (L.) A. Gray, Clearweed. July–Sep. Moist, wooded ravines.

Verbenaceae, Vervain Family

Phryma leptostachya L., Lopseed. June–Sep. Woods.

Phyla lanceolata (Michx.) Greene, Northern frog fruit. May–Sep. Moist or shallow wet areas; horse pasture; disturbed areas.

Verbena stricta Vent., Hoary vervain. May–Sep. Horse pasture; disturbed hill prairies.

Verbena urticifolia L., White vervain. June–Oct. Wet opening in woods; horse pasture; roadsides.

Violaceae, Violet Family

Hybanthus concolor (T. F. Forst.) Spreng., Green violet. Apr–June. Rich, moist woods.

Viola pubescens Aiton var. *eriocarpa* Nutt., Smooth yellow violet. Apr–May. Moist woods.

Viola rafinesquii Greene, Johnny-jump-up. Mar–May. Native to Eurasia. Horse pasture.

Viola sororia Willd., Common violet. Mar–May. Woods.

Viola triloba Schwein. var. *dilatata* (Elliott) Brainerd, Cleft violet. Apr–June. Dry woods.

Vitaceae, Grape Family

Ampelopsis cordata Michx., Raccoon grape. May–July. Along creek in horse pasture; moist woods. [*Ampelopsis* Michx.]

Parthenocissus quinquefolia (L.) Planch., Virginia creeper. June–July. Woods; disturbed areas.

Vitis aestivalis Michx., Summer grape. May–July. Moist woods.

Vitis cinerea (Engelm.) Millardet, Sweet winter grape. May–July. Edge of horse pasture.

Vitis riparia Michx., Riverbank grape. May–June. Moist woods.

Vitis vulpina L., Frost grape. May–June. Dry woods; hill prairies.

CHAPTER 9

WOODY PLANTS OF THE PARK

This list names about 57 species extracted from the vascular plants list. It includes perennial plants that develop substantial and persistent woody stems. These are large or small trees, 19 shrub species, and about seven species of woody vines.

CONE-BEARING PLANTS: CONIFERS

CUPRESSACEAE, CYPRESS FAMILY

Juniperus virginiana L., Red cedar. Hill prairies; open woods.

FLOWERING PLANTS: DICOTYLEDONS

ACERACEAE, MAPLE FAMILY

Acer negundo L., Box elder. Apr–May. Moist woods; disturbed areas; roadsides.

Acer saccharum Marshall, Sugar maple. Apr–May. Woods.

ANACARDIACEAE, CASHEW FAMILY

Rhus aromatica Aiton, Fragrant sumac. Mar–May. Dry woods; hill prairies.

Rhus glabra L., Smooth sumac. June–July. Hill prairies; roadsides.

Rhus typhina L., Staghorn sumac. May–July. Old fields; open woods; edges.

Toxicodendron radicans (L.) Kuntze, Poison ivy. May–June. Woods; field edges.

Sugar maple showing its distinctive lobed leaves.

Fragrant sumac, a relative of poison ivy. Its mature fruits are red, not white.

Annonaceae, Custard Apple Family

Asimina triloba (L.) Dunal, Pawpaw. Apr–May. Moist to dry woods.

Aquifoliaceae, Holly Family

Ilex verticillata (L.) A. Gray, Winterberry. May–July. Dry, rocky woods.

Caesalpiniaceae, Senna Family

Gleditsia triacanthos L., Honey locust. May–June. Disturbed bottomland woods.

Gymnocladus dioicus (L.) K. Koch, Kentucky coffee tree. May–June. Moist bottomland woods.

Calycanthaceae, Strawberry-Shrub Family

Calycanthus floridus L., Eastern sweetshrub. May–June. Native to southeastern United States. Moist ravine woods.

Cannabaceae, Hops Family

Celtis laevigata Willd., Sugarberry. Apr–May. Roadsides.

Celtis laevigata var. *smallii* (Beadle) Sarg., Sugarberry. Apr–May. Bottomland woods.

Celtis occidentalis L., Northern hackberry. Apr–May. Ravine woods.

Celtis occidentalis var. *canina* (Raf.) Sarg., Hackberry. Apr–May. Upland woods.

Caprifoliaceae, Honeysuckle Family

Lonicera maackii (Rupr.) Maxim., Bush honeysuckle. May–June. Native to Asia. Disturbed ridge top and lower slope woods.

Sambucus canadensis L., Common elderberry. June–July. Roadsides.

Symphoricarpos orbiculatus Moench, Coral berry. July–Aug. Moist woods.

Viburnum rufidulum Raf., Southern black haw. Apr–May. Moist woods.

Celastraceae, Staff Tree Family

Celastrus scandens L., American bittersweet. May–June. Dry woods.

Euonymus atropurpureus Jacq., Burning bush. June–July. Moist woods.

CORNACEAE, DOGWOOD FAMILY

Cornus drummondii C. A. Mey., Rough-leaved dogwood. May–June. Hill prairies; horse pasture.

Cornus florida L., Flowering dogwood. Apr–May. Woods; edges of horse pasture and hill prairies.

Cornus mas L., Cornelian cherry. Apr–May. Native to southern Eurasia. Rocky lower slope woods.

CORYLACEAE, HAZELNUT FAMILY

Carpinus caroliniana Walter, Blue beech, musclewood. Apr–May. Moist woods.

Ostrya virginiana (Mill.) K. Koch, Eastern hop hornbeam. Apr–May. Moist woods.

EBENACEAE, EBONY FAMILY

Diospyros virginiana L., Persimmon. May–June. Woods.

ELAEAGNACEAE, OLEASTER FAMILY

Elaeagnus angustifolia L., Russian olive. May–June. Native to Eurasia. Disturbed slope woods; planted at extreme north end of park.

The bark of the persimmon tree is easily recognized by its "alligator" texture.

FAGACEAE, OAK FAMILY

Quercus alba L., White oak. Apr–May. Upland woods.

Quercus ×deamii Trel. (probable hybrid of *Q. macrocarpa* and *Q. muhlenburgii*), Deam's oak, Apr–May. Upland woods.

Quercus macrocarpa Michx., Bur oak. Apr–May. Moist woods.

Quercus marilandica Muenchh., Black jack oak. Apr–May. Upland woods.

Quercus muhlenbergii Englem., Yellow chestnut oak. Apr–May. Upland woods.

Quercus rubra L., Red oak. Apr–May. Upland woods.

Quercus stellata Wangenh., Post oak. Apr–May. Upland woods.

Quercus velutina Lam., Black oak. Apr–May. Upland woods.

Hippocastanaceae, Horse Chestnut Family

Aesculus glabra Willd., Ohio buckeye. Apr–May. Along creek in horse pasture.

Hydrangeaceae, Hydrangea Family

Hydrangea arborescens L., Wild hydrangea. June–Aug. On rocks in moist woods.

Juglandaceae, Walnut Family

Carya cordiformis (Wangenh.) K. Koch, Bitternut hickory. May–June. Moist to wet woods.

Carya glabra (Mill.) Sweet, Pignut hickory. Apr–May. Dry woods.

Carya ovalis (Wangenh.) Sarg., Red hickory. Apr–June. Upland woods.

Older shagbark hickory trees have distinctive exfoliating bark.

Carya ovata (Mill.) K. Koch, Shagbark hickory. Apr–May. Upland woods.

Carya texana Buckley, Black hickory. Apr–May. Hill prairie border.

Carya tomentosa (Poir.) Nutt., Mockernut hickory. May–June. Dry to moist woods.

Juglans cinerea L., Butternut. Apr–May. Rich woods.

Juglans nigra L., Black walnut. Apr–May. Rich woods.

Lauraceae, Avocado Family

Lindera benzoin (L.) Blume, Spicebush. Mar–May. Moist ravine woods.

Sassafras albidum (Nutt.) Nees, Sassafras. Apr–May. Woods; borders of hill prairies.

Magnoliaceae, Magnolia Family

Liriodendron tulipifera L., Yellow poplar. Apr–May. Moist ravine woods.

MORACEAE, MULBERRY FAMILY

Maclura pomifera (Raf.) C. K. Schneid., Osage orange. May–June. Native to southwest central United States. Upland and disturbed woods.

Morus rubra L., Red mulberry. Apr–May. Roadsides.

OLEACEAE, OLIVE FAMILY

Fraxinus americana L., White ash. Apr–May. Woods; hill prairies; horse pasture edge.

Fraxinus quadrangulata Michx., Blue ash. Mar–Apr. Hill prairie borders.

PLATANACEAE, PLANE TREE FAMILY

Platanus occidentalis L., Sycamore. Apr–May. Ravine woods; roadsides.

RHAMNACEAE, BUCKTHORN FAMILY

Ceanothus americanus L., New Jersey tea. June–Aug. Dry woods.

ROSACEAE, ROSE FAMILY

Prunus mexicana S. Watson, Wild plum. Late spring. Hill prairie edge; edge of ridge-top parking area.

Prunus munsoniana W. Wight & Hedrick, Wild goose plum. Mar–Apr. Moist bottomland woods.

Prunus serotina Ehrh., Black cherry. May. Upland woods.

Rosa arkansana Porter var. *suffulta* (Greene) Cockerell, Prairie rose. June–July. Hill prairies.

Rosa carolina L., Pasture rose. May–July. Dry woods.

Rosa multiflora Thunb. ex Murray, Multiflora rose. May–June. Native to China and Japan. Disturbed areas.

Rosa setigera Michx., Prairie rose. June–July. Dry woods.

Rubus allegheniensis Porter, Common blackberry. May–June. Woods.

Rubus occidentalis L., Black raspberry. May–June. Woods

Rutaceae, Citrus Family

Ptelea trifoliata L., Wafer ash. May–July. Hill prairies; edge of horse pasture.

Salicaceae, Willow Family

Populus deltoides W. Bartram ex Marshall, Eastern cottonwood. Mar–Apr. Roadsides; disturbed moist areas.

Salix exigua Nutt., Sandbar willow. Apr–May. Streambanks.

Salix nigra Marshall, Black willow. Apr–May. Shallow water; wet ground.

Simaroubaceae, Quassia Family

Ailanthus altissima (Mill.) Swingle, Tree-of-heaven. June–July. Native to Asia. Roadsides.

Staphyleaceae, Bladdernut Family

Staphylea trifoliata Marshall, Bladdernut. Apr–May. Moist, rocky woods.

Tiliaceae, Linden Family

Tilia americana L., American basswood. May–July. Dry woods.

Ulmaceae, Elm Family

Ulmus rubra Muhl., Slippery elm. Feb–Apr. Woods.

Vitaceae, Grape Family

Ampelopsis cordata Michx., Raccoon grape. May–July. Along creek in horse pasture; moist woods.

Parthenocissus quinquefolia (L.) Planch., Virginia creeper. June–July. Woods; disturbed areas.

Vitis aestivalis Michx., Summer grape. May–July. Moist woods.

Vitis cinerea (Engelm.) Millardet, Sweet winter grape. May–July. Edge of horse pasture.

Vitis riparia Michx., Riverbank grape. May–June. Moist woods.

Vitis vulpina L., Frost grape. May–June. Dry woods; hill prairies.

CHAPTER 10

Mammalian Fauna

An earlier official report stated that 19 mammals have been documented in the park. In this list I included more than twice that number (45 species). Based on the known regional and Illinois ranges and habitat preferences, I added all species that one might reasonably expect to find within the park. Many mammal species, especially the smaller ones, will be seldom encountered by visitors. They may be nocturnal, fossorial (underground dwellers), well camouflaged, or quite shy. Many, unseen, will be watching you as you pass by.

Your best chance for sightings will be of gray squirrels and deer. You may also spot an occasional raccoon or opossum. Unfortunately, many of the mammals we see while traveling are what collection specialists label "DOR," meaning found "dead on road." Indeed, our nation's great road system is also extremely efficient at killing small animals. Be observant as you drive and avoid adding to this carnage.

For each species, a brief statement of the Illinois-documented range follows its common and scientific names. A few added notes are given, such as the time of day they are active and their preferred diet. When you see a statement such as "all counties," uniform distribution is not necessarily implied. A species range may be widespread, but densities can be spotty and variable based on specific needs for space (territory), food, and cover, and on the history of their local occurrence.

See also: www.animaldiversity.ummz.umich.edu and naturalhistory. si.edu/mna/main.cfm. Additional information can be found online by searching "mammals of Illinois." See also Wikipedia for fauna of Illinois. (faunas: Hall [(1981) 2001]; Kurta [1995]; Schwartz & Schwartz [1959].)

ORDER MARSUPIALIA

Family Didelphidae: Opossums

Virginia opossum, *Didelphis virginiana*, common, all counties. Are omnivores and mostly nocturnal.

ORDER INSECTIVORA

FAMILY SORICIDAE: SHREWS

Shrews are mostly nocturnal mammals.

Short-tailed shrew, *Blarina brevicauda* Say, common, northern three quarters of the state and south-central counties. They eat snails, invertebrates, small animals, and a few plant materials.

Least shrew, *Cryptotis parva* Say, uncommon, all counties. It eats invertebrates.

Southeastern shrew, *Sorex longirostris* Bachman, common, southern two thirds of the state. Their diet consists of invertebrates, some seeds, and fungi.

FAMILY TALPIDAE: MOLES

Moles are fossorial, but their raised tunnels give away their presence. They eat invertebrates, some seeds, and fungi.

Eastern mole, *Scalopus aquaticus* L., common, all counties.

ORDER CHIROPTERA

FAMILY VESPERTILIONIDAE: BATS

Bats are the only flying mammals. During the day they roost in caves and tree cavities and under loose bark, shutters, shingles, or within shrubs. Around dusk they begin to fly, capturing large numbers of insects by means of echolocation, a kind of radar. When cold weather approaches, many species migrate to caves for winter hibernation.

Big brown bat, *Eptesicus fuscus* Beauvois, common, all counties.

Silver-haired bat, *Lasionycteris noctivagans* Le Conte, common, all counties.

Eastern red bat, *Lasiurus borealis* Müller, common, all counties.

Hoary bat, *Lasiurus cinereus* Beauvois, migrant, all counties.

Gray bat, *Myotis grisescens* Howell, endangered, southwest counties.

Little brown bat, *Myotis lucifugus* Le Conte, common, all counties.

Northern long-eared myotis, *Myotis septentrionalis*, common, all counties.

Indiana bat, *Myotis sodalis* Miller & G. M. Allen, endangered, all counties.

Evening bat, *Nycticeius humeralis* Rafinesque, uncommon, all counties.

Eastern pipistrelle (tri-colored bat), *Pipistrellus subflavus* F. Cuvier, common, all counties.

ORDER LAGOMORPHA

FAMILY LEPORIDAE: HARES AND RABBITS

Eastern cottontail, *Sylvilagus floridanus*, J. A. Allen, common, all counties. Rabbits are diurnal vegetarians.

ORDER RODENTIA

FAMILY CASTORIDAE: BEAVERS

Beavers are our largest rodent. Because of their abilities, such as tree felling and dam making, they are called a "keystone" species. As they enlarge a wetland, they provide habitat and homes for many other species. They are mostly nocturnal. Beavers eat the soft inner parts of tree bark.

Beaver, *Castor canadensis* Kuhl, variable occurrence, most counties.

FAMILY CRICETIDAE: FIELD MICE

Prairie vole, *Microtus ochrogaster* J. A. Wagner, common, all counties. They move about in covered surface runways, eating mostly tubers and seeds.

Woodland vole, *Microtus pinetorum* Le Conte, common, all counties. They stay out of sight by moving through deep leaf litter. Their food habits are similar to those of the prairie vole.

Muskrat, *Ondatra zibethicus* L., common, all counties. Muskrats make small lodges in ponds using cattails and non-woody vegetation. They eat mostly vegetation such as roots and also some small animals.

White-footed deermouse, *Peromyscus leucopus* Rafinesque, common, all counties. Omnivorous, they eat seeds and insects.

Prairie deer mouse, *Peromyscus maniculatus* Wagner, uncommon, all counties. They make nests in a variety of habitats. Diet is similar to that of the white-footed deermouse.

Southern bog lemming (or mouse), *Synaptomys cooperi* Baird, variable occurrence, all counties. They are vegetarians.

Family Muridae: Old World Rats And Mice

These natives of Europe and Asia have moved with humans around the world. They are mostly nocturnal. While surviving in nature they are quite at home in man's buildings, where they often cause serious property destruction.

House mouse, *Mus musculus* L., common, all counties. Omnivorous, they eat seeds, carrion, or any human food.

Norway rat, *Rattus norvegicus* Berkenhout, common, all counties. Excellent foragers, their preferences range from fish to any human food or garbage.

Family Geomydae: Pocket Gophers

Pocket gophers are nocturnal mammals that make tunnels in loose soil; they also eat roots and tubers.

Plains pocket gopher, *Geomys bursarius* Shaw, St. Clair and Madison Counties, and south of Illinois River junction. They eat mostly roots or tubers and occasionally above-ground vegetation.

Family Sciuridae: Squirrels

Southern flying squirrel, *Glaucomys volans* L., common, all counties. Nocturnal, they live in natural tree cavities. Omnivores, flying squirrels prefer seeds, insects, or nuts.

Woodchuck, *Marmota monax* L., common, all counties. Our largest "squirrel," they are diurnal vegetarians that live in underground burrows.

Eastern gray squirrel, *Sciurus carolinensis* Gmelin, common, all counties. Diurnal omnivores, they live in tree cavities or tree nests.

Eastern fox squirrel, *Sciurus niger* L., common, all counties. Similar to the gray squirrels in habits, but they are often found in fields farther away from trees.

Thirteen-lined ground squirrel, *Spermophilus tridecemlineatus* Mitchell. Common in the northern four fifths of the state. They live in burrows and are opportunistic omnivores. They eat seeds, grass, clover, insects, and eggs.

Chipmunk, *Tamias striatus* L., common, all counties. Diurnal, they subsist on seeds and nuts.

Family Zapalidae: Jumping Mice

Meadow jumping mouse, *Zapus hudsonius* Zimmermann, variable occurrence in all counties. Mostly vegetarian, they will eat seeds, berries, grass, and some insects.

ORDER CARNIVORA

Family Canidae: Dogs, Foxes

Coyote, *Canus latrans* Say, common, all counties. Very adaptable, they have expanded their range throughout most of North America in recent decades. Mostly nocturnal, they will eat carrion and are opportunistic omnivores.

Gray fox, *Urocyon cinereoargenteus* Schreber, variable occurrence, all counties. They will eat mostly small animals and some fruit.

Red fox, *Vulpes vulpes* L., common, all counties. Mostly nocturnal, they eat small animals and birds.

Family Felidae: Cats

Bobcat, *Lynx rufus* Schreber, common in wooded areas. Nocturnal and active at dawn and dusk. About twice the size of a house cat, these carnivores eat a variety of other animals. Sightings have increased greatly in the state recently, including several within the park.

Cougar, *Puma concolor* L. Long considered extirpated in Illinois and the eastern United States, sightings are more commonly reported in the state, including the recent shooting of one south of Chicago by a police officer. The animals range from 110 to 180 pounds and are about 6–8 feet nose to tail. They tend to be nocturnal, generalist predators that hunt by stealth and ambush.

Family Mustelidae: Weasels And Relatives

River otter, *Lutra canadensis* Schreber, endangered, variable occurrence. In the Midwest they can be found in wetlands along major rivers. They eat aquatic animals and some plants.

Striped skunk, *Mephitis mephitis* Schreber, common, all counties. Diurnal, they eat carrion, small animals, and some plants.

Long-tailed weasel, *Mustela frenata* Lichtenstein, uncommon, all counties. Nocturnal, they hunt for small animals and carrion.

Mink, *Mustela vison* Schreber, common, all counties. As above, they are nocturnal hunters of small animals and carrion.

Badger, *Taxidea taxus* Schreber, variable occurrence, northern four-fifths of the state. Seldom seen by people, they eat small animals.

FAMILY PROCYONIDAE: RACCOONS

These engaging diurnal animals are opportunistic omnivores; they will sample any unguarded picnic food. They are very flexible in habitat and selection of den sites.

Northern raccoon, *Procyon lotor* L., common, all counties.

ORDER ARTIODACTYLA

FAMILY CERVIDAE: DEER

White-tailed deer, *Odocoileus virginianus* Zimmermann, common, all counties. Deer are diurnal browsers and grazers. More easily noticed these days, their increasing numbers are due to state game management policies that make it more likely that hunters will be successful, thereby encouraging the sales of more hunting licenses. In some parts of the state, population density is sufficiently great that major vegetational changes are taking place in the forest understory.

CHAPTER 11

BIRDS

GUIDE TO THE BIRD WATCHING CHECKLIST FOR PERE MARQUETTE STATE PARK

This information has been accumulated for all seasons of the year and by many observers. Birds, unlike other organisms in this guide, are not always residents. While some species build nests and breed, many others are migrants just passing through. Yet others are seasonal inhabitants, such as eagles, who may build nests later far to the north.

The Checklist was compiled by Helen Westenfeld in cooperation with the Illinois Department of Natural Resources. Common names of the species follow the American Ornithologists' Union (AOU) Checklist, 7th edition. The following table indicates the habitats where bird species are most likely encountered. In addition, the observations are organized by season and relative abundance using the following symbols.

Scored by season:

a	abundant, expected every trip in large numbers in proper habitat
c	common, expected regularly in season and appropriate habitat
u	uncommon, not expected regularly even in the appropriate habitat or season
o	occasional, found only infrequently
r	rare, only 1 to 5 records

The seasons are identified as follows:

Spring	primarily March through May (although some migration may occur in February and June)
Summer	primarily late May through early August
Fall	primarily August through November (although some migration begins as early as late June and continues well into December)
Winter	primarily December through February

Habitat symbols show where birds are *most likely* to be seen:

bg	bare ground (plowed fields, etc.)
cr	crop fields
an	annuals (naturally occurring)
ng	native grasses/prairies
sg	shrub/grass type old field
ts	tree/shrub type old field
ed	edge between forest and open habitat
uh	upland hardwood forest
bh	bottomland hardwood forest
co	coniferous forest/woods
bl	bluffs and road cuts
st	streams and rivers
la	lakes and ponds
ma	marsh (primarily herbaceous vegetation)
sw	swamp (primarily woody vegetation)
ur	urban areas, farmyards, and man-made

Common Name	Habitat	Spring	Summer	Fall	Winter
GREBES					
Pied-billed grebe	ma/la	c	o	c	r
Horned grebe	la			u	u
PELICANS & CORMORANTS					
American white pelican	ma/la			u	
Double-crested cormorant	la/ma	c		c	
BITTERNS & HERONS					
American bittern	ma/la	r	r		
Least bittern	ma/sw	c	c		
Great blue heron	ma/la	c	c	c	o
Great egret	la/ma	c	c	c	r
Snowy egret	la/ma	r		r	
Little blue heron	la/ma	c	c	c	
Cattle egret	ma/la	u		u	
Green-backed heron	ma/la	c	c	c	
Black-crowned night-heron	sw/ma	u	u	u	
Yellow-crowned night-heron	ma/sw	c	c	c	

WATERFOWL					
Tundra swan	la			r	
Greater white-fronted goose	la/ma	u		u	
Snow goose	la/ma	a		a	a
Canada goose	la/ma	c		a	a
Wood duck	st/sw	a	a	a	o
Green-winged teal	la/ma	c		c	o
American black duck	la/ma	u		u	r
Mallard	ma/la	a	a	a	a
Northern pintail	la/ma	c		c	u
Northern shoveler	la/ma	c		c	
Gadwall	la/ma	c		c	r
American wigeon	ma/la	c	c	c	u
Canvasback	la/st	c		o	c
Redhead duck	la/st	c		c	o
Ring-necked duck	la	c		c	u
Greater scaup	la/st	r		r	
Lesser scaup	la/st	c		c	r
Common goldeneye	la/st	c		o	c
Bufflehead	la/st	c		c	u
Hooded merganser	la/sw	o		o	o
Common merganser	la/st	c			c
Red-breasted merganser	la	r		r	r
Ruddy duck	la	c		c	u
VULTURES, HAWKS, EAGLES & FALCONS					
Turkey vulture	uh/bl	c	c	c	
Osprey	la/st	c		c	
Bald eagle	la/st	c		c	c
Northern harrier	ng/cr	u		u	
Sharp-shinned hawk	uh/ed	o		u	u
Cooper's hawk	uh/bh	u	u	u	u
Northern goshawk	uh/bh			o	o
Red-shouldered hawk	bh	u		u	
Broad-winged hawk	uh	c	c	c	
Red-tailed hawk	uh/ed	c	c	c	c
Rough-legged hawk	cr			u	u
Golden eagle	la	r		r	r

American kestrel	ed	c	c	c	c
Merlin	ed/ng			r	
Peregrine falcon	la/ma	r			r
Prairie falcon	ng/cr				r
UPLAND BIRDS					
Wild turkey	uh/bh	c	c	c	c
Northern bobwhite	ed/cr	c	c	c	c
RAILS, GALLINULES & COOTS					
King rail	ma	r	r	r	
Sora	ma/la	c	c	u	
Common moorhen	ma	r	r	r	
American coot	ma/la	a	o	c	r
SHOREBIRDS					
Black-bellied plover	bg/ma	r		r	
Lesser golden plover	bg/la	r		r	
Semipalmated plover	la/ma	c		c	
Killdeer	bg/la	c	c	c	o
Greater yellowlegs	ma/la	c		c	
Lesser yellowlegs	ma/la	c		c	
Solitary sandpiper	ma/la	u	u	u	
Willet	la/ma	r		r	
Spotted sandpiper	st/la	u	u	c	
Semipalmated sandpiper	ma/la	c		c	
Western sandpiper	ma/la	r		r	
Least sandpiper	ma/la	c		c	
White-rumped sandpiper	ma/la	r		r	
Baird's sandpiper	ma/la	r		r	
Pectoral sandpiper	ma/la	c		c	
Dunlin	ma/la	r		r	
Stilt sandpiper	ma/la	o		o	
Buff-breasted sandpiper	ma/la			r	
Short-billed dowitcher	ma/la	o		o	
Common snipe	ma	c		c	r
American woodcock	ed/bh	c	c		
Wilson's phalarope	la/ma	r		r	
Red-necked phalarope	la/ma			r	
Franklin's gull	la/cr	u		u	

Bonaparte's gull	la/st	u		u	
Ring-billed gull	la/st	a	o	a	a
Herring gull	la/st	c		c	a
Caspian tern	la/st	c		c	
Common tern	la/st	u		u	
Forster's tern	la/ma	u		u	
Black tern	la/ma	c		c	
DOVES & CUCKOOS					
Rock dove	ur/cr	c	c	c	c
Mourning dove	ed/ts	a	a	a	c
Black-billed cuckoo	uh/ts	u		u	
Yellow-billed cuckoo	uh/ed	c	c	c	
OWLS					
Eastern screech-owl	uh/bh	c	c	c	c
Great horned owl	uh/bh	c	c	c	c
Barred owl	bh/uh	c	c	c	c
Long-eared owl	co/ed				r
Short-eared owl	ng				r
Northern saw-whet owl	ts/ed				r
NIGHTJARS & GOATSUCKERS					
Common nighthawk	ur/bg	o	o		
Whip-poor-will	uh/bh	c	c		
SWIFTS & HUMMINGBIRDS					
Chimney swift	ur	c	c	c	
Ruby-throated hummingbird	ed/uh	c	c	c	
KINGFISHERS					
Belted kingfisher	st/la	c	c	c	c
WOODPECKERS					
Red-headed woodpecker	ed/uh	c	c	c	c
Red-bellied woodpecker	uh/bh	c	c	c	c
Yellow-bellied sapsucker	uh/bh	u	u	u	u
Downy woodpecker	uh/bh	a	a	a	a
Hairy woodpecker	uh/bh	c	c	c	c
Northern flicker	ed/uh	a	c	c	c
Pileated woodpecker	bh/uh	c	c	c	c
FLYCATCHERS					
Olive-sided flycatcher	ed/uh	u		u	

Eastern wood-pewee	uh/bh	c	c	c	
Yellow-bellied flycatcher	uh/bh	o		o	
Acadian flycatcher	bh	c	c	u	
Willow flycatcher	ts/ed	u		u	
Least flycatcher	ed/ts	c		c	
Eastern phoebe	st/bh	c	c	c	
Great crested flycatcher	uh/bh	c	c	c	
Eastern kingbird	ed/ts	c	c	c	
LARKS & SWALLOWS					
Horned lark	bg/cr	c		c	
Purple martin	ur/la	o		o	
Tree swallow	la/ma	c	r	c	
Northern rough-winged swallow	bl/st	c	c	c	
Bank swallow	st	u		u	
Cliff swallow	bl/st	o		o	
Barn swallow	ur/ma	c	c	c	
JAYS & CROWS					
Blue jay	uh/bh	a	a	a	a
American crow	uh/cr	c	c	c	c
CHICKADEES & TITMICE					
Black-capped chickadee	uh/bh	a	a	a	a
Tufted titmouse	uh/bh	a	a	a	a
NUTHATCHES & WRENS					
Red-breasted nuthatch	co/uh	c		c	
White-breasted nuthatch	uh/bh	a	a	a	a
Brown creeper	bh/uh	c		c	u
Carolina wren	bh/uh	c	c	c	c
Bewick's wren	ur/ed	r			
House wren	ed/ur	u	u	u	
Winter wren	st/bh	r		r	o
Sedge wren	ng/ma	u	c	u	
Marsh wren	ma	r	r	r	
GNATCATCHERS					
Golden-crowned kinglet	co/bh	c		c	u
Ruby-crowned kinglet	uh/bh	c		c	r
Blue-gray gnatcatcher	uh/bh	c	c	c	

THRUSHES

Eastern bluebird	ts/ed	c	c	c	c
Veery	uh/bh	c		u	
Gray-cheeked thrush	uh/bh	c		u	
Swainson's thrush	uh/bh	c		c	
Hermit thrush	uh/bh	u	u	u	u
Wood thrush	uh/bh	c	c	o	
American robin	ur/ed	a	a	c	c

MIMICS

Gray catbird	ts/ed	c	c	c	
Northern mockingbird	ts/ed	c	c	c	
Brown thrasher	ts/ed	c	c	c	r

WAXWINGS

Cedar waxwing	ts/ed	c	c	c	c

SHRIKES & STARLINGS

Loggerhead shrike	ed/ts	r	r	r	
European starling	ur	a	a	a	a

VIREOS

White-eyed vireo	ts/ed	c	c	c	
Solitary vireo	uh/bh	c		u	
Yellow-throated vireo	uh/bh	c	c	c	
Warbling vireo	bh/ed	c	c	c	
Philadelphia vireo	uh/bh	u		u	
Red-eyed vireo	uh/bh	c	c	c	

WOOD WARBLERS

Blue-winged warbler	ts/ed	c	c	u	
Golden-winged warbler	ts/ed	u		u	
Tennessee warbler	uh/bh	c		c	
Orange-crowned warbler	ts/nh	u		u	
Nashville warbler	uh/bh	c		c	
Northern parula	bh/st	c	c	u	
Yellow warbler	ts/bh	c	c	u	
Chestnut-sided warbler	ed/ts	c		c	
Magnolia warbler	bh/uh	c		u	
Cape May warbler	uh/co	r		r	
Yellow-rumped warbler	uh/bh	c		c	
Black-throated green warbler	uh/bh	c		c	

Blackburnian warbler	uh/bh	c		c	
Yellow-throated warbler	bh/st	o	o	o	
Pine warbler	co/uh	u		u	
Prairie warbler	ts	c	c	u	
Palm warbler	ts/bh	c		c	
Bay-breasted warbler	uh/bh	u		u	
Blackpoll warbler	uh/bh	u		u	
Cerulean warbler	bh/st	u		u	
Black-and-white warbler	uh/bh	c		c	
American redstart	bh	c	c	c	
Prothonotary warbler	st/sw	c	c	c	
Worm-eating warbler	uh/bh	c	c	c	
Ovenbird	uh/bh	c	o	c	
Northern waterthrush	st/sw	c		o	
Louisiana waterthrush	st/bh	c	u	u	
Kentucky warbler	bh/uh	c		c	
Mourning warbler	bh/uh	r		r	
Common yellowthroat	ts/ed	c	c	c	
Hooded warbler	uh/bh	r		r	
Wilson's warbler	ts/ed	o		o	
Canada warbler	ts/bh	u		u	
GROSBEAKS, FINCHES & SPARROWS					
Yellow-breasted chat	ts/ed	c	c	c	
Summer tanager	uh/bh	c	c	u	
Scarlet tanager	uh/bh	c	u	u	
Northern cardinal	ed/ur	a	a	a	a
Rose-breasted grosbeak	uh/bh	c	u	u	
Blue grosbeak	ts/ed	o	o	o	
Indigo bunting	eg/ts	a	a	a	
Dickcissel	ed/ng	c	c	c	
Rufous-sided towhee	ts/ed	c	c	c	u
American tree sparrow	ts/ed	c			c
Chipping sparrow	ed/ur	a	a	a	
Field sparrow	sg/ed	a	a	c	r
Vesper sparrow	cr/sg	o		o	
Lark sparrow	ed/sg	u	u	u	
Savannah sparrow	ng/an	u		u	r

Le Conte's sparrow	ng/ma	o		o	
Fox sparrow	ed/bh	c		c	o
Song sparrow	ed/ts	c	c	c	c
Lincoln's sparrow	ed/bh	u		u	r
Swamp sparrow	ma/sw	c		u	u
White-throated sparrow	ed/bh	c		c	c
White-crowned sparrow	ts/ed	c		c	u
Dark-eyed junco	ed/ur	a		c	c
MEADOWLARKS, BLACKBIRDS & ORIOLES					
Bobolink	ng	u		u	
Red-winged blackbird	ma/cr	a	a	a	c
Eastern meadowlark	ng/cr	c	c	c	o
Rusty blackbird	bh/cr	u		u	c
Common grackle	ed/ts	a	a	a	c
Brown-headed cowbird	ed/uh	a	a	c	u
Orchard oriole	ts/ed	c	c	u	
Northern oriole	bh/ed	a	a	c	
Purple finch	uh/ed	c		c	u
Pine siskin	ur	u		u	u
American goldfinch	ts/ur	a	a	a	c
Evening grosbeak	ur/ed	r		r	r
WEAVER FINCHES					
House sparrow	ur	a	a	a	a
Eastern tree sparrow	ur	u	u	u	u

CHAPTER 12

AMPHIBIANS AND REPTILES

In the absence of previous listings of these animals for the park, the illustrated state field guide by Phillips et al. (1999) was the main source. The animals listed below have been documented in Jersey County, or nearby, and might be expected to be here. This group of animals is frequently overlooked unless one is specifically searching for them. Many live in or around water. The list below includes 17 amphibian species and 42 reptile species. The two venomous snake species are listed, with comments, at the end.

Keep in mind that any small animal, if handled, may bite. Even if the animal is not poisonous, all bites that break the skin are septic and potential infection sites. It is best not to handle any small animal.

Common in the wildlife news these days are stories of a worldwide die-off or serious decline in amphibian populations. As many as one fifth of the approximately 6000 species have become extinct. Beyond the obvious reports of habitat destruction, many other causes have been suggested, including an infectious fungus of the chytrid group. So far there are no reported precipitous losses in Illinois, although there has been a steady decline in populations since the 1980s.

Websites offer more information and have been available from the Illinois Natural History Survey (INHS), the Illinois Department of Natural Resources (IDNR), and other sources, but seem to change frequently. Try searching for Illinois herps, amphibians, snakes, or lizards.

CLASS AMPHIBIA

ORDER CAUDATA: SALAMANDERS

Family Ambystomatidae

Small-mouth salamander, *Ambystoma texanum*

Tiger salamander, *Ambystoma tigrinum*

Family Plethodontidae

Long-tail salamander, *Eurycea longicauda*

Four-toed salamander, *Hemidactylium scutatum*

Family Proteidae

  Mudpuppy, *Necturus maculosus*

Family Sirenidae

  Lesser siren, *Siren intermedia*

ORDER ANURA: FROGS AND TOADS

Family Bufonidae

  American toad, *Bufo americanus*

  Fowler's toad, *Anaxyrus fowleri*

Family Hylidae

  Northern cricket frog, *Acris crepitans*

  Gray tree frogs, *Hyla chrysocelis* and *H. versicolor*

  Spring peeper, *Pseudacris crucifer*

  Western chorus frog, *Pseudacris triseriata*

Family Ranidae

  Plains leopard frog, *Rana blairi*

  Bullfrog, *Rana catesbeiana*

  Green frog, *Lithobates clamitans*

  Pickerel frog, *Rana palustris*

  Southern leopard frog, *Rana sphenocephala*

CLASS REPTILIA

ORDER TESTUDINES: TURTLES

Family Chelydridae

  Snapping turtle, *Chelydra serpentina*

  Alligator snapping turtle, *Macroclemys temminckii*

Family Emydidae

  Painted turtle, *Chrysemys picta*

  Common map turtle, *Graptemys geographica*

  Ouachita map turtle, *Graptemys ouachitensis*

False map turtle, *Graptemys pseudogeographica*

River cooter, *Pseudemys concinna*

Eastern box turtle, *Terrapene carolina*

Ornate box turtle, *Terrepene ornata*

Slider, *Trachemys scripta*

Family Kinosternidae

Eastern mud turtle, *Kinosternon subrubrum*

Musk turtle, *Sternotherus odoratus*

Family Trionychidae

Smooth softshell turtle, *Trionyx muticus*

Spiny softshell turtle, *Apalone spinifera*

ORDER SQUAMATA, SUBORDER SAURIA: LIZARDS

Family Anguidae

Slender glass lizard, *Ophiosaurus attenuatus*

Family Phrynosomatidae

Fence lizard, *Sceloporus undulatus*

Family Scincidae

Ground skink, *Scincella lateralis*

Five-lined skink, *Eumeces fasciatus*

Broadhead skink, *Eumeces laticeps*

Family Teiidae

Six-lined racerunner, *Cnemidophorus sexlineatus*

ORDER SQUAMATA, SUBORDER SERPENTES: SNAKES

Family Colubridae

Worm snake, *Carphophis amoenus*

Racer, *Coluber constrictor*

Ringneck snake, *Diadophis punctatus*

Corn snake, *Elaphe guttata*

Rat snake, *Elaphe obsoleta*

Fox snake, *Elaphe vulpina*

Eastern hognose snake, *Heterodon platirhinos*

Prairie kingsnake, *Lampropeltis calligaster*

Common kingsnake, *Lampropeltis getula*

Milk snake, *Lampropeltis triangulum*

Plain-bellied water snake, *Nerodia erythrogaster*

Diamondback water snake, *Nerodia rhombifer*

Northern water snake, *Nerodia sipedon*

Rough green snake, *Opheodrys aestivus*

Graham's crayfish snake, *Regina grahamii*

Brown snake, *Storeria dekayi*

Redbelly snake, *Storeria occipitomaculata*

Western ribbon snake, *Thamnophis proximus*

Plains garter snake, *Thamnophis radix*

Common garter snake, *Thamnophis sirtalis*

Smooth earth snake, *Virginia valeriae*

Family Viperidae (Venomous)

Compared to most other snakes you might see, species in this family have a more triangular head leading to an abrupt distinction between head and body. They have a heat-sensing pit near their eyes that allows them to detect their prey, which are usually small rodents. Their styles of hunting are called ambush predation.

Both of our venomous snakes have a distinctive banded pattern of scales on the body that can vary somewhat among populations. Also, their skin coloration may become quite a bit darker with age. Pit vipers tend to move away from humans, but sometimes they freeze, which is basically a camouflage tactic. Most people are bitten by getting too close or by accidentally stepping on one. Nearly everyone survives a bite, but medical attention should be sought quickly. Frequently they do not give a full injection, or may give a dry bite without venom. Antivenin kits are available, but some people develop an allergic reaction to that medication. Personally, in decades of hiking in this park, I have never seen either of these snakes.

Timber rattlesnake, *Crotalus horridus*. Members of this species tend to be found in upland woody, often rocky areas, since their winter hibernation time is spent in rocky bluff crevices. Adults range in length from 3 to 5 feet, and they usually rest or sun themselves in a loosely coiled position. The scaled body shows a pattern of regularly spaced, dark brown to black cross bands, widest on top, and tapering down the sides with zigzag edges. These bands alternate with lighter tan to gray areas. Their tail ends in a bony structure that rattles when they feel disturbed or threatened, but they do not always rattle before striking. When striking they inject venom through their two, hypodermic-like fangs. Their conservation status in Illinois is "threatened."

Copperhead, *Agkistrodon contortrix*. As adults, copperheads reach a length of 2 to 3 feet. Like rattlesnakes they are found in wooded areas or near rocks but also around wetlands. Overall the copperhead's body is pale tan to pinkish. The pattern is diamond-like where deltoid lighter areas alternate with darker, hourglass-shaped figures. They are considered more common than rattlesnakes.

LITERATURE CITED
AND OTHER SOURCES

Trees died that ideas may become immortal.

Anderson, R. C., J. S. Fralish & J. M. Baskin. 2007. Savannas, Barrens, and Rock Outcrop Plant Communities of North America. Cambridge University Press, New York. 484 pp. [A symposium volume that describes the history of these vegetation types.]

Berkson, A. & M. D. Wiant (editors). 2004. Discover Illinois Archeology. Ill. Assoc. Advan. Archeol. Ill. Archeol. Surv. Springfield. 27 pp.

Bland, M. K. & P. D. Kilburn. 1966. Bluff prairie vegetation and soil texture. Trans. Ill. Acad. Sci. 59: 25–28. [Describes the relationship of prairie vegetation to its soil habitat.]

Blasing, T. J. & D. Duvick. 1984. Reconstruction of precipitation history in the North American Corn Belt using tree rings. Nature 307: 143–145. [Tree ring widths are a sensitive proxy for moisture conditions in a given year. The authors describe the extent of mid-19th century drought in the Great Plains.]

Blasingham, E. J. 1956a. The depopulation of the Illinois Indians. Part I. Ethnohistory (3)3: 193–224.

Blasingham, E. J. 1956b. Part II. Concluded. Ethnohistory 3(4): 361–412. [A thorough study, based on original sources, of the fate of our American Indians after European contact.]

Bohlen, H. D. 1989. Birds of Illinois. Indiana University Press, Bloomington. 240 pp.

Braile, L. W., W. J. Hinze, G. R. Keller, et al. 1986. Tectonic development of the New Madrid rift complex, Mississippi embayment, North America. Tectonophysics 131: 1–21. [Describes the buried rift zone dating from late Precambrian times and how it represents a crustal zone of weakness.]

Brugam, R. B., B. Owen & L. Kolesa. 2004. Continental-scale climate forcing factors and environmental change at Glimmerglass Lake in the Upper Peninsula of Michigan. Holocene 14: 807–817. [Describes changes in humidity and climate during the Holocene.]

Butzer, K. W. 1978. Changing Holocene environments at the Koster Site: A geo-archaeological perspective. Amer. Antiq. 43: 408–415. [Environmental variations in the lower Illinois River valley in the past 12,000 years.]

Campos, P. F., E. Willerslev, A. Sher, et al. 2010. Ancient DNA analyses exclude humans as the driving force behind late Pleistocene musk ox (*Ovibos moschatus*) population dynamics. Proc. Natl. Acad. Sci. U.S.A. 107: 5675–5680. [The genetic variation of the musk ox is tracked from DNA samples accumulated from Siberian Pleistocene deposits.]

Carpenter, G. W. 1967. Calhoun Is My Kingdom. The Sesquicentennial History of Calhoun County, Illinois. Board of County Commissioners, Calhoun County. Dan Merkel Printing. [A brief history of the county's exploration and early settlement.]

Carter, R. W. 1952. Pere Marquette State Park in the History of Illinois. Department of Public Works and Buildings, Division of Parks and Memorials, State of Illinois, Springfield. 61 manuscript pp. [A wide-ranging work that includes much U.S. history beyond the park area.]

Collinson, C. D., H. Swann & H. B. Willman. 1954. Guide to the Structure and Paleozoic Stratigraphy along the Lincoln Fold in Western Illinois. Illinois State Geological Survey Guidebook 3. 75 pp.

Csontos, R. & R. Van Arsdale. 2008. New Madrid seismic zone fault geometry. Geosphere 4(5): 802–813. [Describes the history of the region just to the south beginning with the development of the North American craton in Precambrian times.]

DeJarnett, A. 1993. An Upland Flora of Pere Marquette State Park, Jersey County, Illinois. M.S. Thesis, Southern Illinois University, Edwardsville. [In addition to the descriptive checklist, Dr. DeJarnett's work describes and locates vegetational communities within the park.]

Evers, R. A. 1955. Hill prairies of Illinois. Ill. Nat. Hist. Surv. Bull. 26: 367–446. [The classic study. An especially useful baseline survey on the extent of original prairies. Most sites have been seriously encroached upon by woody vegetation in the past half century.]

Fay, J. & A. C. Fortier. 2007. The Tall Grass Prairie Peninsula: Its Role in Shaping American Culture. Stipes Publishing, Champaign, Illinois. 252 pp. [Unusual breadth: covers ecology, common prairie plants, early human culture and artifacts, even 20th-century jazz history.]

Flint, T. (1918) 1968. Recollections of the Last Ten Years in the Valley of the Mississippi. Southern Illinois University Press, Carbondale, Illinois. 343 pp. [This is a rare and detailed report of travels in this region during 1815–1816.]

Fowler, M. 1971. The origin of plant cultivation in the central Mississippi Valley: A hypothesis. *In* S. Struever (editor), Prehistoric Agriculture. [Cited on p. 164. A description of the earliest stages of plant domestication during the Archaic period.]

Frank, A. J. 1948. Faulting on the northeastern flank of the Ozarks. Geol. Soc. Amer. Bull. 59(12): 1322. [Meeting abstract. Describes how the local eastern course of the Mississippi River is controlled by the Cap au Grès fault system.]

Greene, A. V. 1990. Illinois Geographic Information Systems: An index to automated statewide databases. Ill. State Water Surv. Circ. 175. Illinois State Water Survey, Champaign, Illinois. [A general index, not including detailed data.]

Hall, E. R. (1981) 2001. Mammals of North America. Wiley, New York. 2 vols. 1300 pp. [The authoritative reference on this topic.]

Hamilton, O. B. (editor). 1919. History of Jersey County, Illinois. Munsell, Chicago. [The only compendium of early history as of that date.]

Harris, S. E., Jr., C. W. Horrell & D. Irwin. 1977. Exploring the Land and Rocks of Southern Illinois. A Geological Guide. Southern Illinois University Press, Carbondale, Illinois. 240 pp. [Clearly written, detailed, and well illustrated.]

Hodge, F. W. (editor). 1907, 1910. Handbook of American Indians North of Mexico, parts 1 and 2. Smithsonian Institution. Bureau of American Ethnology. Bulletin 30. Government Printing Office, Washington, D.C. Part 1, 972 pp; part 2, 1221 pp. [A trove of information, with images, regarding tribes, leaders, culture, and treaties, much transcribed from original long-deceased sources.]

Hoffmeister, D. & C. O. Mohr. 1972. Fieldbook of Illinois Mammals. Dover Publications, New York. [A good listing of mammals and their ranges.]

Hopely, A. M. 1967. Blood Sweat and Grafton. Grafton Historical Society, Grafton, Illinois. Third printing, 2011. 37 pp. [Miscellaneous narratives, stories, and photographs.]

Hough, S. E., R. Bilham, K. Mueller, et al. 2005. Wagon loads of sand blows in White County. Seismol. Res. Lett. 76(3): 373–386. [Technical analysis of the 1811–1812 New Madrid earthquakes, as well as those in the Wabash Valley, and Cahokia locations.]

Iseminger, W. 2010. Cahokia Mounds. America's First City. The History Press, Charleston, South Carolina. 174 pp. [Indian cultures interpreted as seen through research at this remarkable site.]

Keating, R. C. 1999. Pere Marquette State Park, Jersey County, Illinois. A field trip guide for the XVI International Botanical Congress, July 31, 1999. 8 manuscript pp. [A brief guide stressing local flora and ecology of two field trip sites.]

Kellogg, L. P. 1917. Early Narratives of the Northwest 1643-1699. Chas. Scribner's Sons, New York. 382 pp. [Source of the Piasa Bird quotation (p. 249), extracted from Thwaites (1900).]

Kilburn, P., B. Tutterow & R. B. Brugam. 2009. The tree species composition and history of barrens identified by government land surveyors in southwestern Illinois. J. Torrey Bot. Soc. 136: 272–283. [Presettlement ecological history reviewed, including the park area.]

King, J. E. 1981. Late Quaternary vegetational history of Illinois. Ecol. Monogr. 51: 43–62. [Records the post-Pleistocene changes in this region.]

King, J. E. 1982. Fossils. Illinois State Museum. Story of Illinois. No. 14. 69 pp. [Brief guide to geology, fossil collecting, and the groups of organisms found in the fossil record.]

Kurta, A. 1995. Mammals of the Great Lakes Region. University of Michigan Press, Ann Arbor. 392 pp. [A regional listing with descriptions.]

Lopinot, N. H. & W. I. Woods. 1993. Wood overexploitation and the collapse of Cahokia. Pp. 206–231 in S. M. Scarry (editor), Foraging and Farming in the Eastern Woodlands. University Press of Florida, Gainesville. [An analysis of the wood supplies and their overexploitation around 1150 CE.]

Martin, P. S. 1984. Prehistoric overkill. Pp. 354–403 in P. S. Martin & R. G. Klein (editors), Quaternary Extinctions: A Prehistoric Revolution. University of Arizona Press, Tucson. [Made the case for the idea that early man destroyed the post-glacial megafauna.]

McAdams, W., Jr. 1887. Records of Ancient Races in the Mississippi Valley; Being an Account of Some of the Pictographs, Sculptured Hieroglyphs, Symbolic Devices, Emblems, and Traditions of the Prehistoric Races of America, With Some Suggestions as to Their Origin. Chancy R. Barnes Publishing Company, St. Louis. [The only publication of a self-trained archeologist. His were among the first observations of artifacts in this region.]

McClain, W. E. 1983a. Master Plan for Pere Marquette Nature Preserve, Jersey County, Illinois. Division of Forest Resources and Natural Heritage, Illinois Department of Conservation. 27 manuscript pp. [While the study targets the park's 297.4-acre nature preserve in the northern part of St. Andrew ridge, it contains background on the general park area.]

McClain, W. E. 1983b. Photodocumentation of the loss of hill prairies within Pere Marquette State Park, Jersey County, Illinois. Trans. Ill. Acad. Sci. 76: 343–346.

McClain, W. E. & E. A. Anderson. 1990. Loss of hill prairie through woody plant invasion at Pere Marquette State Park, Jersey County, Illinois. Nat. Area. J. 10(2): 69–75. [Describes the loss of hill prairie coverage over many decades.]

McClain, W. E. & J. E. Ebinger. 2007. Fire maintained, closed canopy barren communities in western Illinois. Trans. Ill. Acad. Sci. 100: 209–221. [Describes these natural communities and the effect of European settlement on that vegetation type.]

McClain, W. E. & J. E. Ebinger. 2012. Flora of Twin Shelters and Twin Mounds hill prairies, Pere Marquette State Park, Jersey County, Illinois, changes since 1963. Trans. Ill. Acad. Sci. 105: 11–18. [Their inventory documents the loss of about 10% of the prairie flora of these sites in the past 50 years.]

Milulic, D. G. & J. Kluessendorf. 1999. Silurian geology and the history of the stone industry at Pere Marquette State Park and Grafton, IL. Illinois Association of Aggregate Producers. Teachers' Workshop Guide Book, Part 1, Pere Marquette State Park. 17 pp. [Brief outline of local history, plus a road log of local geology stressing the earliest (Silurian) strata.]

Mueller, K., S. E. Hough & R. Bilham. 2004. Analysing the 1811–1812 New Madrid earthquakes with recent instrumentally recorded aftershocks. Nature 429(May): 284–288. [Instrumentation is used to reconstruct the epicenter of this quake and its relationship to the southeastern Illinois quakes.]

Nelson, J. C., A. Redmond & R. E. Sparks. 1994. Impacts of settlement on floodplain vegetation at the confluence of the Illinois and Mississippi rivers. Trans. Ill. Acad. Sci. 87(3/4): 117–133. [A comparison of pre- and post-settlement vegetation ecology, including results of the 1938 closing of Lock and Dam 26 that permanently raised river levels.]

Nelson, W. J. 1995. Structural Features in Illinois. Department of Natural Resources. Ill. Geol. Surv. Bull. 100. 144 pp. [Detailed illustrated guide to strata and fault zones in the state.]

Pauketat, T. R. 2004. Ancient Cahokia and the Mississippians. Cambridge University Press, New York. 218 pp. [A detailed description of this topic and its regional context.]

Phillips, C. A., R. A. Brandon & E. O. Moll. 1999. Field Guide to Amphibians and Reptiles of Illinois. Illinois Natural History Survey, Urbana, Illinois. 292 pp. [This is the most comprehensive guide including photographs and key characters.]

Pielou, E. C. 1992. After the Ice Age. The Return of Life to Glaciated North America. University of Chicago Press, Chicago. 376 pp. [A description of the changes in climate and vegetation after melting of the ice sheets.]

Ragan, V. M. 1999. 46th Annual Field Trip. Association of Missouri Geologists. Kansas City, Missouri. [Describes some geological strata in eastern Missouri that are similar to strata in this park.]

Reed, C. A. 1970. Extinction of mammalian megafauna in the Old World Late Quaternary. Bioscience 20: 284–288. [A broad review of events of this period.]

Reinertsen, D. L. & J. D. Treworgy. 1991. Guide to the Geology of the Pere Marquette State Park area, Jersey County. Field Trip Guidebook, October 26, 1991, Department of Energy and Natural Resources, Illinois State Geological Survey. 34 pp + figures and maps. [Contains descriptions, maps, and road logs for this region.]

Robertson, K. R., M. W. Schwartz, J. W. Olson, et al. 1995. Fifty years of change in Illinois hill prairies. Erigenia 14: 41–52. [Analyzes the changes (losses) in hill prairies along the bluffs since the 1930s.]

Rowling, F. (editor). 2011. The Road to Grafton. Construction of the Great River Road into Grafton, Illinois. Grafton Historical Society, Grafton, Illinois (no pagination). [A collection of vintage photographs and appendices.]

Rubey, W. W. 1952. Geology and mineral resources of the Hardin and Brussels quadrangles, Illinois. US Geological Survey Professional Paper 218. 179 pp. [Summarizes the surface and underlying geology of the region.]

Schwartz, C. W. & E. R. Schwartz. 1959. The Wild Mammals of Missouri. University of Missouri Press, Columbia. 341 pp.

Schwegman, J. 1973. Comprehensive plan for the Illinois Nature Preserves System. Part 2. The Natural Divisions of Illinois. Illinois Nature Preserves Commission, Rockford. 32 pp + map. [This detailed map, based on regional flora and ecology, has become the standard working document.]

Seid, M. J. & J. A. Devera. 2008. Bedrock geology of Brussels Quadrangle. Calhoun and Jersey Counties, Illinois. Illinois Geological Survey, Champaign, Illinois. 7 pp. [A clearly written description of the strata and structure of this region, but some geological background is assumed.]

Shook, B. A. S. & D. G. Smith. 2008. Using ancient mtDNA to reconstruct the population history of northeastern North America. Amer. J. Phys. Anthropol. 137: 14–29. [Native Americans of central Illinois, before European contact, had northeastern roots extending back at least 3000 years.]

Squires, D. 2001. The great Midwest quake. Illinois Country Living 13, 6 pp. [Movement of the New Madrid fault in 1811–1812 is described in its geological and social context.]

Stelle, L. J. 1993. Post-glacial environments in East-central Illinois. Center for Social Research. Parkland College, Champaign, Illinois. 48 pp. [Good description of this landscape. Search online for Stelle Parkland, and you'll find a number of papers on this and related topics.]

Struever, S. (editor). 1971. Prehistoric Agriculture. American Museum of Natural History, Paperback. [A collection of papers on this topic. See example by Fowler, cited previously.]

Surovell, T. A. & B. S. Grund. 2012. The associational critique of Quaternary overkill and why it is largely irrelevant to the extinction debate. Amer. Antiq. 77(4): 672–687. [A discussion of the coexistence of humans and megafauna and their different ecological requirements.]

Theler, J. L. & R. F. Boszhardt. 2003. Twelve Millennia. Archeology of the Upper Mississippi River Valley. University of Iowa Press, Iowa City. 254 pp. [While stressing territory north of here, it offers a good summary of wider climatic, geological, and cultural issues.]

Thwaites, R. G. 1900. Jesuit Relations 59: 139–143. [Source of quotations from Marquette's journals.]

Tikrity, S. S. 1968. Tectonic Genesis of the Ozark Uplift. Ph.D. Dissertation, Washington University, St. Louis. 196 pp + 6 maps. University Microfilms (now ProQuest LLC) #69-9013. [The most complete review and study of the structural geology to the southwest of this park.]

Titterington, P. F. 1935. Certain bluff mounds of western Jersey County, Illinois. Amer. Antiq. 1(1): 6–46. [Includes an account of the work of William D. McAdams and his early archeological investigations.]

Treworgy, J. D. 1981. Structural Features in Illinois—A Compendium. ISGS Circular 519. Illinois State Geological Survey, Champaign.

Van der Pluijm, B. A. & P. A. Catacosinos. 1996. Basement and Basins of Eastern North America. Geol. Soc. N. Amer. 209 pp. [Papers from a conference at Ann Arbor, Michigan, Fall 1993.]

Walters, J. C., J. R. Groves & S. Lundy. 2004. From Ocean to Ice: An Examination of Devonian Bedrock and Overlying Pleistocene Sediments. Blackhawk County, Iowa. Geological Society of Iowa. Guidebook 75. [Detailed study of the Devonian Cedar Valley Formation.]

Warner, K. L. 1998. Water-quality Assessment of the Lower Illinois River Basin: Environmental Setting. USGS, Department of the Interior, Urbana, Illinois. 50 pp. [In addition to water, much information on soils, climate, wetlands, and geology.]

White, J. & M. H. Madany. 1978. Classification of natural communities in Illinois. Pp. 310–405 in J. White, Illinois Natural Areas Inventory, Vol. 1. Survey Methods and Results. Department of Landscape Architecture, University of Illinois, Urbana. [Illinois natural communities described.]

White, S. V. 1900. Reminiscences of Jersey County, Illinois from 1835 to 1850. (Delivered at Chautauqua, Illinois, at a "Reunion of Early Settlers of Jersey County"). State Archives 977.385W588.

Wiens, J. J., D. D. Ackerly, A. P. Allen, et al. 2010. Niche conservatism as an emerging principle in ecology and conservation biology. Ecol. Lett. 13: 1310–1324. [A study of the relation between species traits and changing environments.]

Wiggers, R. 1997. Geology Underfoot in Illinois. Mountain Press Publishing, Missoula. 304 pp. [Thirty-seven geologically interesting sites for the state are described and illustrated, including a good chapter on this park.]

Yin, Y. & J. C. Nelson. 1997. Bottomland hardwood forests along the upper Mississippi River. Nat. Area. J. 17: 164–173. [A history of the upper river woody flora in the face of human-induced changes in the 19th century that including logging and impoundments.]

Index, General Topics

tree rings 23
Tucker, J. 35
Tucker Knob 26, 40, 74
turtles 21, 46
Twin Mounds 49, 84, 87
Twin Mounds prairies 49
Twin Peaks 44, 79
Twin Shelter 87
Twin Springs 73, 81

U

understory trees 42, 44–45, 87–88, 91, 108, 116, 118
Upper Louisiana 34
Upper Park Road 3, 16, 94–95
USDA Soil Conservation Service 88

V

Vadalabene Bike Trail 7, 97

vegetation 22, 25, 39, 41–43, 46, 48, 51, 66, 84, 92, 140–141, 145
vegetation types 42
venomous snake 92, 153, 156
visitor center 1, 3, 5, 7, 17–18, 55, 57–58, 74, 80–81, 84–85, 88, 98–99, 112, 127

W

Wabash Valley fault 65
Warford Road 99
War of 1812 34
wet-mesic upland forest 45
white ash 86
White County 65
white oak 89–91
wildfires 48
Williams Hollow 75, 82–83, 86, 91, 98–99

Williams, W. 35
Wisconsinan 21, 23, 67–69, 74
Wisconsinan glaciation 23, 68
witness trees 43
woodland 80, 93, 103, 105, 113, 122, 125
wooly mammoth 20

X

xeric conditions 46

Y

yellow oak 82
Younger Dryas 22–23
Younger Dryas cooling period 22

Z

Zea mays 27

Index of Plants and Animals

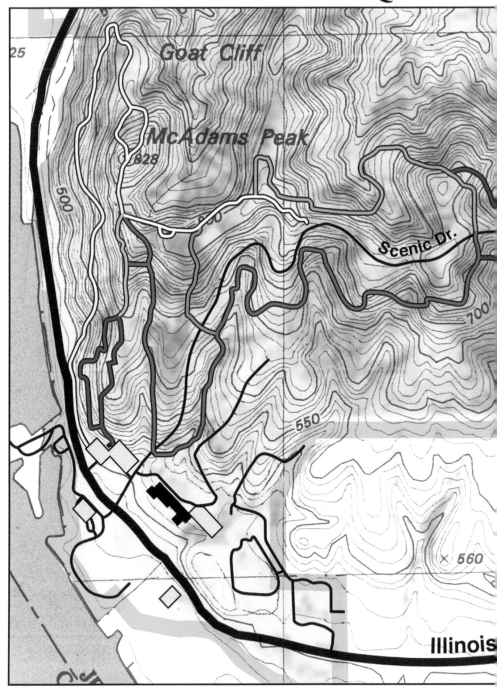

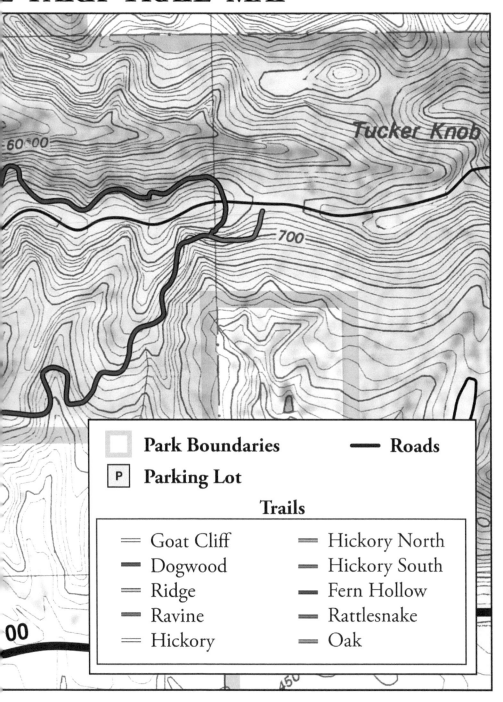

E PARK TRAIL MAP

Tucker Knob

60 00

700

| | Park Boundaries | — Roads |
| P | Parking Lot | |

Trails

=	Goat Cliff	=	Hickory North
—	Dogwood	—	Hickory South
=	Ridge	—	Fern Hollow
=	Ravine	=	Rattlesnake
=	Hickory	=	Oak

00

450

CPSIA information can be obtained
at www.ICGtesting.com
Printed in the USA
BVHW021240080219
539563BV00002B/1/P